Credits

Acquisitions Editor
Aaron Black

Project Editor
Christopher Stolle

Technical Editor
Dennis Cohen

Copy Editor
Scott Tullis

Editorial Director
Robyn Siesky

Business Manager
Amy Knies

Senior Marketing Manager
Sandy Smith

Vice President and Executive Group Publisher
Richard Swadley

Vice President and Executive Publisher
Barry Pruett

Project Coordinators
Patrick Redmond
Lynsey Stanford

Graphics and Production Specialists
Joyce Haughey
Andrea Hornberger
Jennifer Mayberry

Quality Control Technician
Lauren Mandelbaum

Proofreading and Indexing
Cindy Lee Ballew/
Precisely Write
BIM Indexing &
Proofreading Services

Screen Artists
Ana Carrillo
Jill A. Proll

Illustrators
Ronda David-Burroughs
Cheryl Grubbs

About the Author

Lonzell Watson is the award-winning author of *Teach Yourself Visually iPhoto '09* and of other popular titles, including *Teach Yourself Visually Digital Video, Canon VIXIA HD Digital Field Guide, Final Cut Pro 6 for Digital Video Editors Only,* and *Final Cut Express 4 Essential Training* from Lynda.com. Lonzell is an Apple Certified professional and is a full-time technical author and instructional designer whose courseware has been used to train the CIA, FBI, NASA, and all branches of the U.S. Armed Forces.

He is a frequent contributor to StudioMonthly.com and is the owner of Creative Intelligence LLC, an instructional design and technical writing company (creativeintel.com). He holds a master's degree in Instructional Design and Development from Bellevue University.

Author's Acknowledgments

I would like to give special thanks to Aaron Black and Jody Lefevere, without whom this project would not have been possible. I would also like to thank the artists in the Wiley graphics department for their amazing work articulating complex concepts through fantastic visual works of art. You guys never cease to amaze me. I would also like to thank technical editor Dennis Cohen for overseeing the accuracy for exercises in this book as well as the terminology.

Special thanks go to Laura Clor, my lovely wife Robyn, Shannon Johnson, Danya and Sean Platt, and Kimmi and James Patterson for their assistance as I wrote this book. I would also like to thank my dad, Henry Edward Watson, who passed away during the writing of this book. He taught me how to work, how to succeed in life, and how to lead by example. He will forever remain in my heart. This book is dedicated to him.

How to Use This Book

Who This Book Is For

This book is for the reader who has never used this particular technology or software application. It is also for readers who want to expand their knowledge.

The Conventions in This Book

① Steps

This book uses a step-by-step format to guide you easily through each section. Numbered steps are actions you must do; bulleted steps clarify a point, step, or optional feature; and other steps give you the result.

② Notes

Notes give additional information — special conditions that may occur during an operation, a situation that you want to avoid, or a cross-reference to a related area of the book.

③ Icons and Buttons

Icons and buttons show you exactly what you need to click to perform a step.

④ Tips

Tips offer additional information, including warnings and shortcuts.

⑤ Bold

Bold type shows command names, options, and text or numbers you must type.

⑥ Italics

Italic type introduces and defines a new term.

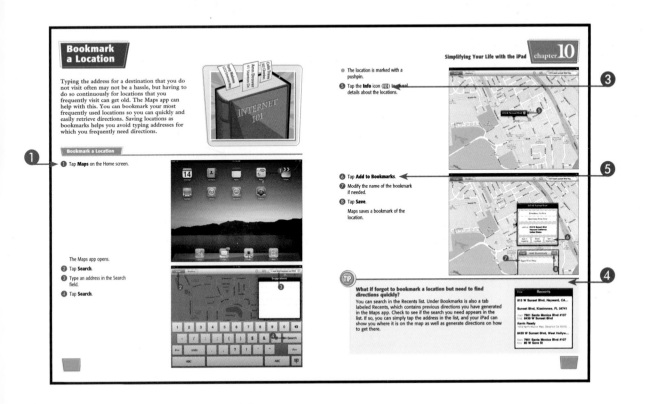

Table of Contents

chapter 1 Exploring the iPad

Take a Look at the iPad 4

Discover iPad Features.. 6

Start Up and Log In 8

Explore the iPad Home Screen 10

Explore Important iPad Settings 12

chapter 2 Understanding What You Can Do with Your iPad

Experience the Web.. 16

View, Organize, and Share Your Photos............................... 18

Email Friends 20

Organize Your Contacts and Appointments........................... 21

Create Professional Documents 22

Enjoy Music and Videos... 24

Download Apps and eBooks... 26

Navigate with Maps 28

Accessorize Your iPad 30

chapter 3 Configuring the iPad

Customize the Home Screen.. 34

Reset the Default Home Screen Layout 36

Protect Your iPad with a Passcode 38

Configure the iPad's Sleep Setting 40

Turn Sounds On and Off 42

Customize the Home Button 43

Adjust the Brightness of the Screen 44

Turn Off Wi-Fi or Switch to Airplane Mode 45

Change the iPad Wallpaper 46

Configure Parental Controls 48

Reset the iPad 50

Cutting, Copying, and Pasting Editable and Non-Editable Text 52

Copy and Paste a Photo 54

Search Your iPad by Using Spotlight 56

chapter 4   **Getting the Most from the Internet**

Understand Internet Access 60

Connect to a Wi-Fi Network for the First Time 62

Activate Your 3G Service 64

Change the Default Search Engine 66

Manage Multiple Web Browsers 68

Explore Web Browser Security and Privacy Options 70

Bookmark Your Favorite Websites 72

Explore Touch-Screen Navigation Tips 74

Turn On AutoFill 76

View an RSS Feed 78

Table of Contents

chapter 5   Maximizing Email on the iPad

Learn about Managing Email Accounts 82

Add an Email Account for the First Time 84

Create a New Email Account 86

Specify the Default Email Account 88

Switch to Another Email Account 90

Disable an Email Account 92

Use a Different Server Port 94

Configure Authentication for Outgoing Mail 96

Automatically Check for New Emails 98

Email a Link to a Webpage 100

Set Message Font Size 102

Create a Custom iPad Signature 104

Disable Remote Message Images 106

chapter 6   Syncing the iPad

Connect Your iPad to a Computer 110

Prevent Your iPad from Syncing Automatically 112

Sync Your Contacts List 114

Sync Your Calendar 116

Sync Your Email Account 118

Sync Your Bookmarks 120

Sync Music and Music Videos 122

Sync Podcasts 124

Sync Audiobooks 126

Sync TV Show Episodes 128
Sync Photos on Your Computer with Your iPad 130
Save Photos from Emails 132
Import Photos from Your Camera 134

chapter 7   Getting the Most from iTunes and Photos

Discover What You Can Do with iTunes 138
Buy and Download in iTunes 140
Subscribe to Podcasts 142
Rate Content in the iTunes Store 144
Configure iPad Audio Settings 146
Browse and Play Content in the iPod App 148
Create a Standard Playlist in the iPod App 150
Play Videos, Movies, and TV Shows 152
Customize Video Settings 154
View Photos on Your iPad 156
Send a Photo by Email 158
Create a Custom Slideshow 160

chapter 8   Getting the Most from YouTube and iBooks

Explore YouTube 164
Locate Videos on YouTube 166
Save a Video as a Favorite 168
Email a Link to a Video 170
Understand iBooks Features 172
Purchase and Download eBooks 174

Table of Contents

chapter 9 Managing Contacts and Appointments

Create a New Contact 178

Edit an Existing Contact 180

Assign an Email Address to a Contact. 182

Assign a Web Address to a Contact 184

Assign a Physical Address to a Contact. 186

Create a Custom Label for a Contact 188

Add Extra Fields for a Contact. 190

Add Notes to a Contact 192

Add Photos to Contacts 194

Add Appointments to Your Calendar 196

Edit an Existing Appointment 198

Set Up a Repeating Event. 200

Convert an Event to an All-Day Event. 202

Add an Alert to an Event 204

chapter 10 Simplifying Your Life with the iPad

Explore Accessibility Options for the Visually and Hearing Impaired. 208

Display Your Current Location by Using Maps 210

Get Directions by Using Maps. 211

Specify a Location When You Do Not Have an Address 212

Display a Contact's Location 214

Bookmark a Location. 216

Learn about MobileMe 218

Set Up a MobileMe Account on Your iPad. 220

Configure MobileMe Synchronization on the iPad 222

The Monarch butterfly appears every Spring, the best known of all butterflies.

Configure MobileMe Synchronization on Your Mac 224

Set Up MobileMe on Your PC 226

Send Photos to Your MobileMe Gallery 228

Explore iWork 230

chapter **11** **Enhance Your iPad with the App Store**

Explore the App Store 234

Download Free Apps 236

Purchase and Download Apps from the App Store 238

Move Apps from Your Computer to Your iPad 240

Check for Updates to Apps 242

chapter **12** Maintaining and Troubleshooting the iPad

Update iPad Software 246

Back Up and Restore Your iPad's Data and Settings 248

Learn to Extend Battery Life 250

Troubleshoot Connected Devices 252

Troubleshoot the Inability to Charge the iPad Battery 254

Troubleshoot Wi-Fi Problems with Wi-Fi Accessibility 256

Troubleshoot Why iTunes May Not See Your iPad 258

Troubleshoot the Inability to Sync with iTunes 260

CHAPTER 1

Exploring the iPad

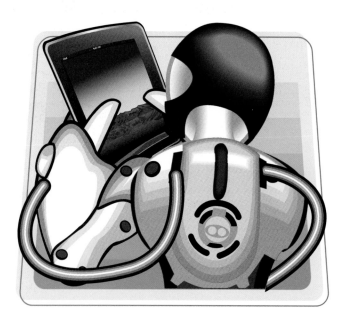

This chapter acquaints you with one of the most highly anticipated electronic devices of all time: the iPad. The iPad is an amazingly powerful work of technological art, renowned for its large, high-resolution, multi-touch screen and overall sleek design. In this section, I give you an extensive tour of the many features that have made the iPad the talk of the town. I also discuss some ideas about how to customize those features to suit your own personal needs.

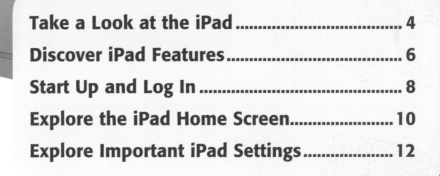

Take a Look at the iPad 4

Discover iPad Features 6

Start Up and Log In 8

Explore the iPad Home Screen 10

Explore Important iPad Settings 12

Take a Look at the iPad

The iPad is elegantly designed, easy to use, and amazingly powerful. The iPad is capable of performing many of the tasks that you may require from your MacBook, MacBook Pro, or PC, including surfing the web, exchanging emails, desktop publishing, downloading apps, and playing video games. It is important that you become familiar with the iPad hardware so you can take advantage of everything the iPad offers.

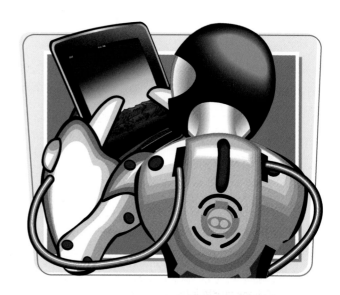

iPad Overview

The iPad is a portable hardware device that is a hybrid between the iPhone and a laptop. The large LED backlit display acts as both monitor and keyboard. The iPad operating system and multi-touch screen is based on the same technology used on the iPhone, where you use gestures to scroll, rotate, and zoom in on objects. Almost every iPhone app in the App Store works on the iPad.

iPad Technical Specifications

The iPad has a 9.7-inch screen and a 1024 × 768 pixel resolution at 132 pixels per inch. The iPad uses a 1GHz Apple A4 custom processor and comes in three storage capacities: 16GB, 32GB, and 64GB flash drives. The iPad can access Wi-Fi networks as well as cellular networks with its 3G model.

iPad Design and Buttons

● Multi-Touch Screen

You use the touch screen to access everything on the iPad with just a tap of your finger. Gestures are used to scroll, rotate, and zoom in on objects on-screen. The display is also used to view content in portrait or landscape orientation when you physically turn it.

● Home Button

The Home button acts as a starting point for many of the functions you perform with the iPad, including bringing the iPad out of Sleep mode, accessing Spotlight, and returning you to the Home screen.

● Headphone Jack

You can insert your own personal headphones into the headphone jack to listen to music, watch videos, and play games in privacy.

● On/Off, Sleep/Wake

You can use this button in conjunction with the Home button to turn off the iPad. You can press this button to place the iPad into Sleep mode and to bring the iPad out of Sleep mode.

● Mute

You can use the Mute button as a quick and easy way to mute all sounds on the iPad.

● Volume Up/Down

You can use the Volume Up/Down buttons to raise and lower the volume of the iPad.

● 30-Pin Connector

The 30-pin connector enables you to attach the iPad to the iPad dock in order to charge it. You can use this connector to connect to a computer as well as connect to other iPad accessories, such as the iPad camera connection kit.

● Built-In Speaker

The built-in speaker enables the iPad to play back audio without accessories, such as headphones or external speakers.

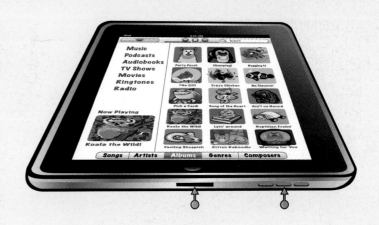

Discover iPad Features

The iPad is an entertainment center as well as a productive office tool. It is important that you understand the key features of the iPad so you can best plan how it can serve you.

Learn about Battery Life

The iPad has up to ten hours of battery life. Battery life can vary wildly depending on the tasks you perform. Watching videos and playing games uses more power than playing music. Higher brightness levels for the display screen can also use more battery life.

Connect to Wi-Fi and 3G Networks

The iPad has the ability to take advantage of the fastest Wi-Fi networks. The iPad can automatically detect available Wi-Fi networks that you can join. The iPad is also available in a 3G model, so if you happen to be somewhere without a Wi-Fi network, you can still access the web.

Use Accessories for the iPad

Many accessories have been made for the iPad, such as protective cases; the keyboard dock, which features a full-sized keyboard; a stand-alone dock; and a camera connection kit for importing photos from a camera or SD card. The iPad also comes with Bluetooth 2.1 + EDR technology, allowing you to use devices such as wireless headphones and the wireless keyboards.

Play Videos

You can watch HD movies, TV shows, podcasts, and music videos on the high-resolution iPad screen. You can switch between widescreen and full-screen viewing just by double-tapping the viewing area. You can control downloaded videos by using simple player controls, including Rewind, Play, Pause, and Fast Forward, or by simply jumping to the next or previous scenes.

Shop the App Store

The App Store provides you with tens of thousands of apps that you can choose from to enhance the capabilities of your iPad. By tapping the App Store icon on the Home screen, you can choose from almost 140,000 apps (at the time this is being written), ranging from games to business apps, that enable you to take full advantage of your iPad. An important thing to note here is that currently, the vast majority of apps available are made specifically for the iPhone and iPod touch. The number of iPad-specific apps is growing by the day.

Buy, Download, and Read eBooks

The iPad is also an eReader, with access to thousands of books, ranging from classics to bestsellers, through the iBooks app, Kindle app, Stanza, and other eReaders you can download. Once you download a book, the iBooks app places it on your virtual bookshelf. You can choose books from your bookshelf and read them in sharp clarity, even in low light. You will need to download the free iBooks app from the App Store.

Find Your Way by Using Maps

The iPad also comes with a very helpful Maps app that provides high-resolution maps that can help you find directions. You can pinpoint your current location, bookmark locations, get up close with street view, and even search for nearby landmarks. The Maps app is powered by Google.

Take Notes, Schedule Appointments, and Work with Contacts

The iPad also comes with apps that can help you schedule appointments and manage contacts. You also have the ability to sync the data within these apps to your Mac or Windows PC. The Notes, Calendar, and Contacts apps are great ways for you to stay organized when you are on the go.

Start Up and Log In

Starting your iPad is a very straightforward process that simply involves pressing the Home button. To access the iPad features, you will then need to unlock it. Powering on and off the iPad is an incredibly easy process.

Learn about the Home Button

The Home button acts as a starting point for many of the functions you perform with the iPad, and you can also customize its functionality. Its most basic functions are to wake the iPad from sleep and to turn off the iPad while pressing the sleep/wake switch in conjunction. You can press the Home button to bring the iPad out of Standby mode so you can unlock the iPad. You also use the Home button to return to the Home screen. Press and hold the Home button to access the Voice Control screen. You can customize what the Home button does when you double-press it.

Unlocking the iPad

When the iPad is asleep, it is considered locked, rendering any taps on the touch screen and the volume controls unresponsive. This is to protect the iPad from any unwanted taps. After you turn on the iPad or bring it out of Sleep mode, you reach the Slide to Unlock screen. Like the iPhone or iPod touch, you can place a finger on the Arrow button and slide it to the right to unlock the iPad.

Protecting Your iPad with a Passcode

Unfortunately, simply locking your iPad is not sufficient for protecting your personal effects. Others can also unlock your iPad. You can protect your iPad by designating a passcode that one must type before he or she can gain access to your iPad. It is a good idea to protect your iPad with a passcode if you have sensitive or confidential information on your iPad. See Chapter 3 for more on setting a passcode for your iPad.

Shutting Down and Sleeping

You can power down your iPad by pressing the On/Off button located on the upper-right corner of the iPad. You can put your iPad in Sleep mode by pressing the Sleep/Wake button, which also happens to be the On/Off button. Putting the iPad to sleep locks the iPad.

Explore the iPad Home Screen

The iPad Home screen is the gateway to nearly all the activities you can engage in on the iPad. It is important for you to know the components of the Home screen so you can navigate your iPad.

● Home Screen

The Home screen is the starting point for almost everything you can do on the iPad. On the Home screen, you can see and access the icons for all the apps installed on the iPad. You can customize the appearance of the Home screen by changing the wallpaper to another Apple design or specify a graphic of your own as wallpaper. You can also rearrange the app icons and distribute them across multiple Home screen pages. You can always reset the Home screen layout. See Chapter 3 for more on resetting the Home screen layout for your iPad.

● Dock

The Dock gives you quick access to the apps you use the most, such as Safari, Mail, Photos, and iPod. You can rearrange the order of the icons located on the Dock, but you cannot delete the preinstalled apps located on it. You can also remove the preinstalled apps from the Dock onto the Home screen and put different apps on the Dock. Tap any of the icons on the Dock to open the specified app.

App Icons

The icons located on the Home screen represent the apps installed on the iPad. The apps that come preinstalled on the iPad cannot be deleted. You can only move them. Each time you download a new app from the App Store, a new icon appears on the Home screen, which you can move or delete/uninstall. Press your finger on the app that you want to move until the icons start to wiggle. You can then drag the icon to a new location or you can tap the ⊗ to delete it.

Pages

Located at the bottom of the Home screen, just above the Dock, are multiple small dots signifying that more screens are located on the desktop. You can navigate between these pages by sliding the touch screen to either the left or right with your finger. You can also tap a dot to move forward or backward through pages. Initially, there are only two dots: one being the Home screen and the leftmost for Spotlight. Each time that you fill up an entire page with app icons, a new page is created. You can also drag an existing icon off-screen to manually create new pages. The dot for the current page is filled with white.

Explore Important iPad Settings

Your iPad provides you with many options for customization, including accessibility options and parental controls. Understanding your iPad's settings can help you get the most from your iPad.

Learn about Accessibility Options

The iPad possesses features that make it more accommodating for people who may be visually impaired, be hard of hearing or deaf, or have a physical or learning disability. The iPad is equipped with a screen reader and support for the playback of closed-captioned content and other helpful universal access features.

Explore Parental Controls

If children have access to your iPad or if they have one of their own, the iPad has parental control features that can help you restrict the content they are exposed to on the web. You can restrict their access to popular social networking sites, such as YouTube, and even restrict their downloading capabilities from the App Store and iTunes.

Learn about Airplane Mode

While on a plane, you must deactivate any device that may receive phone calls, wireless messaging, and Internet access. When you travel, you can place the iPad into Airplane mode, which disables its wireless abilities, therefore making it an approved device while in flight. While in Airplane mode, you can enjoy previously downloaded content, such as music, videos, and eBooks, during your flight. Airplane mode is only available on the 3G model. The Wi-Fi will need to be disabled on the Wi-Fi model.

Restore iPad Default Presets

If you have spent a lot of time configuring your iPad and would like to return it to its previous state, such as when you first purchased it, you can always reset it to the default settings. If you ever want to sell your iPad, consider resetting the iPad so no one has access to your personal data, such as your contacts, emails, and appointments. You can choose to erase all content and settings when you reset the iPad. See Chapter 3 for more on resetting your iPad.

Understanding What You Can Do with Your iPad

Are you ready to learn more about what you can do with your iPad? This chapter introduces you to many of the activities you can engage in on the iPad, ranging from entertainment to productivity. You also learn how to put the many features of the iPad to work for you in your daily life.

Experience the Web 16

View, Organize, and Share Your Photos 18

Email Friends 20

Organize Your Contacts and
      Appointments 21

Create Professional Documents 22

Enjoy Music and Videos 24

Download Apps and eBooks 26

Navigate with Maps 28

Accessorize Your iPad 30

Experience the Web

The iPad offers many of the web-browsing features that you have become accustomed to with a Mac or Windows PC. You can browse the web with Safari, manage multiple browser pages, and exchange email with family and friends. Understanding the iPad's web features can help you gain the most from your web experience.

Surf the Internet with Safari

The iPad is equipped with a large multi-touch screen so you can view webpages as they were intended. The iPad is equipped with the Safari web browser so you can visit your favorite place on the web by navigating with your fingertips. You can scroll through pages by flicking your finger up, down, left, and right on-screen, and you can pinch photos to zoom in and out.

Manage Multiple Browser Pages

The iPad makes it easy for you to open multiple web browser windows at the same time, load different pages into them, and navigate between the multiple pages. You can view multiple open pages in a grid, enabling you to move quickly between pages with just the tip of your fingers. The ability to manage multiple browser pages enables you to perform multiple searches without losing your previous search.

Email Family and Friends

You can compose new emails by using the iPad's large on-screen keyboard and delete messages with a simple tap. You can view photo attachments in messages, and you save them via the built-in Photos app. The iPad also allows you to view your email in various ways according to how you hold the iPad. When you hold the iPad in landscape orientation, you can view your email as a split screen displaying both open email and messages in your Inbox. You can view an open email by itself by holding the iPad in the portrait orientation. See Chapter 5 for more on maximizing email on your iPad.

View, Organize, and Share Your Photos

The iPad's high-resolution screen is perfect for viewing your photos. The iPad offers a variety of ways to import photos, showcase your photos, and share them with others. Understanding your options enables you to take full advantage of your still images on the iPad.

Import Photos

The iPad does not have a camera to take photos. But you can sync your photos from your computer, download them from email messages and webpages, or import them directly from your camera by using the optional camera connection kit. Once you have put your photos on your iPad, you can organize them, showcase them, and email them to friends and family.

View Photo Albums

Similar to iPhoto or Photoshop Elements, the iPad enables you to organize groups of photos into albums. The Photos app displays the photos on your iPad as if they were placed in a stack. You can tap on a stack to open a particular album of photos to view. You can easily view your photos by scrolling though the albums, tapping on photos to enlarge them, and also rotating and zooming in to photos.

Play Slide Shows

You can showcase your photos on the iPad by setting up slideshows that include transition effects and background music. You can customize your slideshows by choosing the transition effects, designating the amount of time a slide appears on-screen, and setting the slideshow to Shuffle to display album photos in random order. The iPad speakers make for great slideshows with your favorite music in the background. See Chapter 7 for more on creating slideshows on your iPad.

Email Photos

You can mail photos on your iPad as attachments to share them with friends and family. Once received, recipients can view your photos from within their email and then download them to their hard drive to place them in their own collection. Emailing photos is a quick and simple way to exchange your favorite photos with others. See Chapter 5 for more on emailing photos on your iPad.

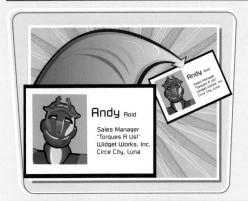

Assign Photos to Contacts

Do you forget faces? You can take a picture with a camera of an individual for whom you have contact information and then assign that picture to that contact. This way, when you thumb through your contacts, you see a face associated with the contact information and you will never forget a face. You can assign photos to contacts from a photo album or by way of the Contacts app itself.

Use the iPad as a Picture Frame

The iPad's 9.7-inch display, surrounded by a sleek black frame, showcases photos in crisp, vibrant color. You can use your iPad as a beautiful picture frame while it is charging. The iPad uses motion sensor technology that allows it to sense the orientation in which it is being held. Whether your photos are in portrait or landscape orientation, you can position the iPad in the correct orientation to ensure that photos look their best.

Email Friends

Email is a very simple and popular way to stay in contact with friends and family. By understanding email options with the iPad, you can best maximize your email experience.

View Your Email

The iPad uses motion sensor technology to allow you to view your email in various ways depending on how the iPad is positioned. In landscape orientation, the iPad displays your email as a split screen, showing both open email and messages in your Inbox. By holding the iPad in the portrait orientation, you can view your open email and also your Inbox.

Manage Email Accounts

The iPad comes with a Mail app that is a scaled-back and streamlined version of what you may be accustomed to on a standard Mac. With that being said, the Mail app offers features that are very effective in managing your email while on the move. You can set up your iPad with one or more email accounts that you already use on your computer, giving you quick and easy access. The iPad recognizes five email services: Microsoft Exchange (Hotmail), MobileMe, Google Gmail, Yahoo Mail, and AOL. You can also configure POP and IMAP accounts. See Chapter 5 for more on adding email accounts to your iPad.

Email Links to Websites

The iPad makes it easy for you to share links to interesting websites that you may come across with family and friends. You can send a link via email with just a few taps. Some sites include an option to email a link, but in the absence of such an option, the iPad also gives you the alternative of copying and pasting the link into an email. The ability to email links makes it easy for you to share your findings on the web.

Create a Custom Signature

For those of you who may have never used an email signature, it is a block of text added to outgoing emails. You have probably seen them at the bottom of emails you have received; they can range from a short—such as "Cheers"—to a long quote. The iPad Mail app affords you the same ability as the default mail program on your Mac or Windows PC to customize your own email signature.

The iPad is not just an entertainment device; it is also equipped with apps that can help you be more productive. Becoming familiar with the Notes, Contacts, and Calendar apps can help you organize your day.

Take Notes

The iPad makes it easy for you to write down impromptu thoughts and messages with the Notes app. Instead of relying completely on memory, you can jot down notes by using the iPad's large on-screen keyboard to save each message. When holding the iPad in the landscape orientation, you can see the virtual note-taking pad as well as a list of all your notes. The iPad circles the current note in red so you instantly know where you are in the list.

Manage Contacts

You can keep a virtual Rolodex of all the important business contacts that you make by using the Contacts app. The Contacts app makes finding names, numbers, and other important information easier. A new view enables you to see both the contact list and a single contact at the same time. You can even tap the address for a contact to open Google Maps and get directions. See Chapter 9 for more on creating contacts on your iPad.

Schedule Appointments

You can pencil in appointments and keep track of your day-to-day schedule by using the Calendar app. You can view your calendar by day, by week, by month, or even in list view. You can also see an overview of an entire month or a single day in detail. The iPad can display more than one calendar at a time so you can manage both your work and family schedules. See Chapter 9 for more on adding appointments in the Calendar app on your iPad.

Create Professional Documents

iWork is Apple's productivity software suite, which includes Keynote, Numbers, and Pages. You can purchase each iWork app separately for $9.99 each. Understanding the purpose of each piece of software can help you decide if iWork can make you more productive.

Explore Keynote

Keynote makes it easy for you to create high-quality, professional presentations with a few taps of your finger. The Keynote app enables you to choose from professionally designed template themes to create your presentation. You can customize each presentation slide by swapping placeholder text and graphics with your own words and images. Choose from elements such as tables, charts, media, and shapes to add the finishing touches to your slides.

Explore Pages

Pages offers advanced tools for writing and easy page layout by using a collection of Apple-designed templates. You can use Pages to create high-quality résumés, brochures, school reports, or invitations. Pages enables you to add tables and charts to display important data in your documents as well as copy data from other iWork apps, namely Numbers.

Explore Numbers

Numbers makes it easy for you to quickly create high-quality, attractive spreadsheets. Use the high-quality Apple-designed templates and the easy-to-create formulas, tables, and charts to help you organize and plan. You can use Numbers to assist you with planning an event, saving for retirement, tracking your diet, and even keeping a journal.

Purchase iWork for the iPad

Each iWork app has been redesigned for iPad so you can create professional presentations, word-processing documents, and spreadsheets with your fingertips. Each app is sold individually for $9.99 in the App Store, but you can also purchase the entire suite at once. The iWork apps are the most powerful productivity apps made for a mobile device, and they are easy to use.

Enjoy Music and Videos

Your iPad is a digital media player and is packed with entertainment possibilities. You can play music, movies, TV shows, podcasts, audiobooks, and videos; read eBooks; view photos; and access YouTube all from the iPad. Understanding your entertainment options can help you take advantage of the iPad's digital media capabilities.

Buy Music, TV Shows, and Podcasts

iPad makes it easy for you to use the iTunes app to preview and download music, TV shows, and podcasts from a vast library of digital content. You can also purchase Books and download hours of free educational content from iTunes U (University). To purchase content from iTunes, you first need to set up an iTunes account. See Chapter 7 for more on purchasing and downloading content from iTunes on your iPad.

Play Music with the iPod App

Your iPad can quickly transform into an iPod by using the iPod app. Simply tap the iPod icon on the Home screen to access your downloaded music, movies, TV shows, and podcasts. For those of you who use the iPod classic or iPod nano, the iPad does not utilize a click wheel to navigate your iPod content but instead uses a set of preset browse buttons, such as the iPhone and iPod touch. Each browse button represents a group of media files that has been

organized in some way, such as Playlists, Artists, Songs, and Videos.

Watch HD Movies and TV Shows

The iPad can quickly transform into a movie screen with no distracting keyboard or buttons on-screen so you can watch downloaded HD movies, TV shows, and other compliant mp4 content. You can view your movies and TV shows by using simple controls, such as Rewind, Play, Pause, and Fast Forward, or by jumping from scene to scene via on-screen controls.

View Videos on YouTube

The YouTube app simplifies your YouTube experience by organizing videos specifically for the iPad device so they are easier to view and navigate. You simply tap a video to play it. When you position the iPad in landscape orientation, the video automatically plays in full screen.

Mange Your Music, Videos, and Podcasts

If you have plenty of music, videos, and other content on your iPad, you need some way to manage all that content. The iPod app is a great media-management apps that can help you make sense of it all. To get the most from these apps, you need to start by properly labeling and cataloging content so it can be quickly located and accessed.

Download Apps and eBooks

The iPad has access to literally thousands of apps that can increase its functionally by way of the App Store. By exploring what the App Store has to offer, you can make better decisions on what types of apps may work best for you.

Enhance Your iPad with the App Store

If the iPad does not possess some of the functionality you would like, there may be an app for that. You can browse the App Store by category, such as Games, Entertainment, Utilities, Social Networking, Music, and Productivity. The list is too long to list them all here. There are many free apps as well as more advanced apps that you have to pay for that you can download wirelessly to your iPad. To purchase apps in the App Store, you must have an iTunes Store account. See Chapter 5 for more on purchasing and downloading apps from the App Store on your iPad.

Download Video Games

The App Store has many games for you to download and play on your iPad — some free and some that you have to pay for. Many of these games are specifically designed to take advantage of the iPad's motion sensor technology, allowing you to tilt the iPad to control aspects of the game on-screen. Most of the games for the iPhone and iPod touch can be played on the iPad.

Sync Apps to Your iPad from Your Mac

You cannot play downloaded apps from the App Store on you computer, but if you have purchased apps on your Mac or PC, you can sync those apps to your iPad as well as your iPhone or iPod touch. A simple cable, namely the USB to Dock cable, can connect your iPad to your Mac or PC to sync programs such as games, eBook readers, productivity apps, and even social networking apps. You can choose to sync automatically or manually, which allows you to pick and choose the apps you want to sync.

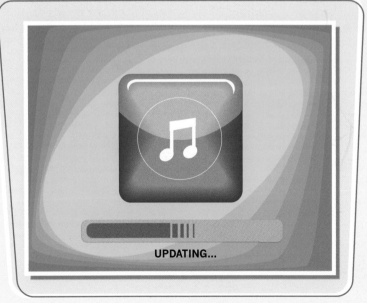

UPDATING...

Update Your Apps

As software developers continue to work on improving their apps, they often release updates to the software you may have already downloaded from the App Store. The App Store notifies you when developers have released an update for the software you have previously downloaded by placing a red alert on the App Store icon located on the Home screen. The alert signifies how many apps have updates by displaying a number. You can simply access the App Store and choose Updates to initiate the updates. You can choose to update individual apps or update each of them automatically.

The Maps app on the iPad gives you the ability to find locations, get directions, and pinpoint locations. Maps on the iPad can also provide up-to-date traffic information so you can choose the best route. By exploring what the Maps app can do for you, you can utilize it for your own purposes.

Display Your Current Location by Using Maps

The Maps app can help you pinpoint your exact location if you should ever find yourself in an unfamiliar location. You can simply tap the Maps icon located on the Home screen and then tap the Tracking button to have Maps show your precise current location. The location is represented by a blue dot on a detailed map. You can use the map to find another location or just to know where you are in relation to other destinations.

Get Directions

The Maps app can help you get from point A to point B by providing you accurate directions. You can get step-by-step driving, walking, and public transportation directions to a specified destination by typing the addresses for the starting location and desired destination. You can also get directions for locations in your Contacts list by tapping your friends' names into the destination field instead of an actual address. See Chapter 10 for more on getting directions with the Maps app on your iPad.

Specify a Location

The Maps app can also help you find locations for which you do not have an address. For example, you may know that a specific restaurant is located downtown, but you do not know how to get to downtown from your hotel. The Maps app enables you to add a pushpin where downtown is located on the map and then generate directions on how to get there.

Bookmark Locations

Typing the address for a destination that you do not often visit may not be a hassle, but having to do so continuously for locations that you frequently visit can get old. The Maps app can help with this. You can bookmark your most frequently used locations so you can retrieve directions quickly and easily. Saving locations as bookmarks helps you avoid typing addresses for which you frequently need directions. See Chapter 10 for more on learning how to bookmark locations within the Maps app on your iPad.

Display a Map of a Contact's Location

You can display a map of a contact's location by using both the Contacts and the Maps apps. Simply tap a contact's physical address in the Contacts list to display a detailed map with street names and the destination marked with a pushpin.

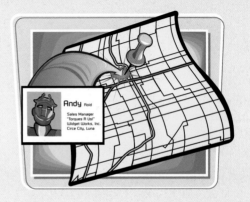

Accessorize Your iPad

Optional accessories for the iPad can help you protect your iPad, give you the flexibility of typing with an actual keyboard, and offer the benefit of a handy camera connection kit. By understanding what iPad accessory options are available, you can choose the accessories that work best for you.

Protect Your iPad with the iPad Case

Much like the iPhone and iPod, the iPad also has optional protective cases that help prevent it from becoming scratched or collecting dust. The iPad case not only protects the iPad, but it can also be used to situate the iPad in various positions so it is easy to type, view photos, and watch movies for extended periods of time.

Charge Your iPad with the iPad Dock

You can purchase a basic iPad dock to charge and sync your iPad. Keep in mind that the iPad has Bluetooth capability, so you can also purchase a Bluetooth-enabled keyboard to use instead of the on-screen keyboard. It also offers an audio jack. A plain charging dock also comes in handy if you just need an extra charging dock at home or at the office.

Explore the iPad Keyboard Dock

The iPad keyboard dock gives you the added convenience of actually typing with a physical keyboard while charging the iPad. The iPad keyboard dock provides a typing experience more similar to using a computer keyboard. Users who perform extensive writing tasks may find the more tactile iPad keyboard dock a better alternative to the on-screen keyboard. You can also use it to sync your iPad. It also offers an audio jack so you can connect the iPad to a stereo.

Discover the iPad Camera Connection Kit

The camera connection kit is composed of two connectors that can be attached to the iPad dock, allowing the iPad to directly download digital content from electronic devices. One connector allows you to download photos directly from a camera's USB cable, whereas the other allows you to download content from an SD card.

Use the iPad USB Power Adapter

The iPad power adapter is much like the adapter that comes with most Apple hardware. It gives you the flexibility of being able to charge your iPad through an electrical outlet. This may be a good option if you want to use the iPad for extended periods of time without being tethered to a shorter cable. The iPad 10W USB power adapter is 6 feet long.

3

Configuring the iPad

Your iPad is a state-of-the-art entertainment system and productivity tool that can be customized to fit your own specific needs. In this chapter, you discover the variety of settings at your disposal to personalize your iPad and how to optimize them for your everyday life. You learn how to not only customize its appearance but also its functionality, including security settings and parental controls.

Customize the Home Screen...........................34

Reset the Default Home Screen Layout.......36

Protect Your iPad with a Passcode...............38

Configure the iPad's Sleep Setting...............40

Turn Sounds On and Off...................................42

Customize the Home Button...........................43

Adjust the Brightness of the Screen.............44

**Turn Off Wi-Fi or Switch to
    Airplane Mode**...45

Change the iPad Wallpaper............................46

Configure Parental Controls..........................48

Reset the iPad..50

**Cutting, Copying, and Pasting Editable
    and Non-Editable Text**....................................52

Copy and Paste a Photo...................................54

Search Your iPad by Using Spotlight............56

Customize the Home Screen

The Home screen is where you start many of the activities on your iPad. As you purchase new apps for your iPad, the number of icons on the Home screen multiplies, which may prompt you to rearrange some of them. One of the most basic ways to customize your iPad is to rearrange the icons on the screen to your liking.

① Display any page of the iPad Home screen.

Note: *You can achieve this by closing out of whatever app you may currently be in by pressing the* **Home** *button (*⬜*).*

Note: *In this example, I have chosen my second page, which is almost filled with apps I have downloaded.*

② Tap any of the app icons on the Home screen and continue to press until the icons begin to wiggle.

Note: *When the icons begin to wiggle, you can move them around with your finger.*

③ Tap and drag the icon that you want to move to a new location.

Note: The surrounding icons move and adjust around the placement of the icon you drag.

Note: You can even drag the icon off the screen, to the right, to create a new page.

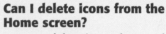

④ Press the **Home** button (⬜).

Your iPad saves the current icon arrangement.

Can I move icons located on the Dock at the bottom of the screen?

Yes. You can press one of the icons on the Dock, and when it starts to wiggle, you can rearrange it on the Dock. You can even remove it from the Dock and replace it with another icon.

Can I delete icons from the Home screen?

You can delete icons that you have downloaded and installed on your iPad. When the icons begin to wiggle, an ⊗ appears in the top-left corner of the icon. You can tap the ⊗ to remove the icon and uninstall the app. Over time, if you find that you do not use certain apps very often, consider moving them to another page or delete them. You cannot delete the preinstalled apps.

Reset the Default Home Screen Layout

Over time, after you have experimented with many different arrangements, you may want to return the Home screen to the default layout. Your iPad makes it easy for you to reset the changes you have made for a fresh new start.

Reset the Default Home Screen Layout

① Display the Home screen.

Note: *You can achieve this by exiting whatever app you may currently be in by pressing the* **Home** *button (⬜).*

② Tap Settings.

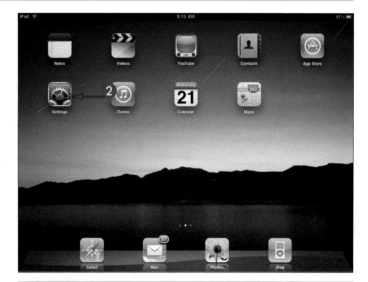

The Settings screen appears.

③ Tap **General**.

④ Tap **Reset**.

The Reset screen appears.

⑤ Tap **Reset Home Screen Layout**.

A dialog box warns you that the Home screen will be reset to the factory default layout.

⑥ Tap **Reset**.

iPad resets the Home screen to the factory default layout.

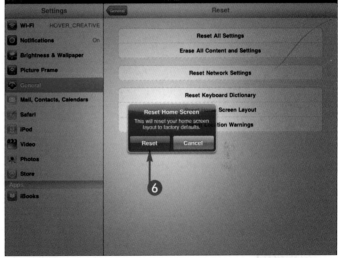

TIP

Is my new app deleted when I reset the Home screen?
No. Resetting the Home screen does not discard any new app you may have added to the Home screen. Only the layout is affected. For example, if you have previously moved the Notes app icon to another page, it is placed back on the first page in its original location. If you moved one of the default app icons from the Dock, it is placed back on the Dock once you reset the Home screen layout.

Protect Your iPad with a Passcode

By default, your iPad is set to lock after a period of inactivity. This protects your iPad from accidental taps while it is in your bag or carried in your hands. Unfortunately, locking your iPad does not protect confidential information that may be on your iPad. When you lay your iPad down, anyone so inclined can unlock your iPad and view your personal information. To keep your sensitive materials private, you can protect your iPad with a four-digit passcode. It is highly important that you remember your passcode.

Protect Your iPad with a Passcode

① Tap **Settings** on the Home screen.

The Settings screen appears.

② Tap **General**.

The General screen appears.

③ Tap **Passcode Lock**.

The Set Passcode screen appears.

④ Tap **Turn Passcode On**.

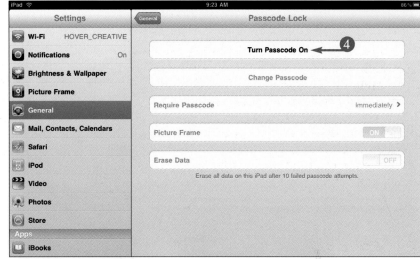

The **Set Passcode** dialog box opens.

⑤ Type your passcode.

iPad prompts you to type the code again.

Note: For security purposes, the code you type is represented in the box with dots.

⑥ Type the passcode again.

The code is now saved, and the Passcode Lock screen appears.

Note: You can tap Require Passcode to specify how much time elapses before your iPad locks and requests the passcode.

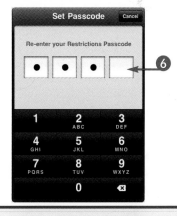

 TIPS

How do I change my passcode?
You can change your passcode from the Passcode Lock screen. You need to know the original code to change it to a new one. Follow these steps:

① Tap **Settings** on the Home screen.

② Tap **General**.

The General screen appears.

③ Tap **Change Passcode Lock**.

④ Type the old passcode.

⑤ Type the new passcode.

Change Passcode

How do I turn off my passcode?
You can turn off your passcode from the Passcode Lock screen. You need to know the original code you set in order to turn it off:

① Tap **Settings** on the Home screen.

② Tap **General**.

③ Tap **Passcode Lock**.

④ Tap **Turn Passcode Off**.

⑤ Type the current passcode.

Turn Passcode Off

Configure the iPad's Sleep Setting

During periods of inactivity, your iPad automatically goes into Sleep mode and locks as a means of conserving battery power and protecting against unwanted taps. You can specify the amount of time that elapses before the iPad goes to sleep. If the default time of one minute is too short, you can change it to a longer amount of time.

① Tap **Settings** on the Home screen.

The Settings screen appears.

② Tap **General**.

The General screen appears.

③ Tap **Auto-Lock**.

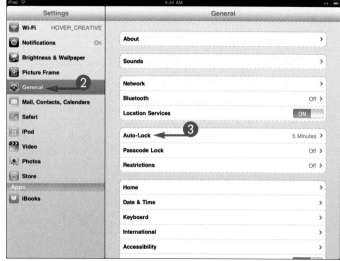

The Auto-Lock screen appears.

④ Tap the interval that you want.

Note: *Your choices are 2 Minutes, 5 Minutes, 10 Minutes, 15 Minutes, and Never.*

iPad saves the new interval.

● The current interval appears with a check mark.

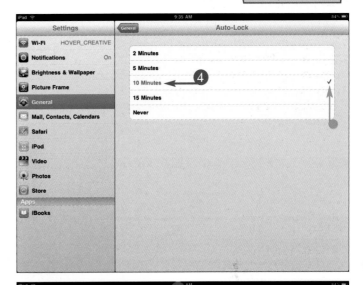

⑤ Tap **General** to return to the General settings screen.

TIP

Anything else I should know about iPad sleep settings?
You should know that you do not have to wait for the iPad to fall asleep on its own; you can manually put your iPad in Sleep mode by pressing the Sleep/Wake button. Consider putting the iPad into Sleep mode after you have finished using it to help conserve battery power. Every little precaution you can take to conserve battery power does have an impact on battery life.

Turn Sounds On and Off

In conjunction with the Volume Up/Down button located on the right side of your iPad in portrait orientation, you also have the ability to turn sounds off altogether. Consider turning off the sounds if you will use your iPad in a meeting where beeps and clicks may be deemed distracting or altogether inappropriate.

1 Tap **General** in the Settings menu.

2 Tap **Sounds**.

The Sounds screen appears.

3 Tap the sounds that you do not want to the **Off** position.

4 Tap **New Mail** to the **Off** position.

When you tap **New Mail** to **Off**, that chime you hear when you receive an email is deactivated.

When you tap **Sent Mail** to **Off**, the swoosh that you hear when you send an email is deactivated.

When you tap **Calendar Alerts** to **Off**, the chime that you hear whenever you receive an event alert is deactivated.

When you tap **Lock Sounds** to **Off**, the click your iPad makes when you lock and use the Slide to Unlock button is deactivated.

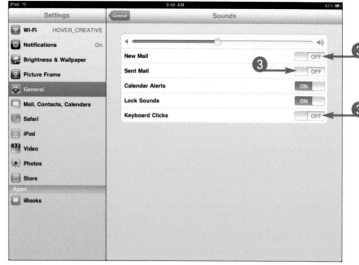

Customize the Home Button

By default, the Home button () of your iPad performs three primary duties. It takes you to the Slide to Unlock screen if you press it when iPad is asleep; if you press it when the iPad is on, it returns you to the Home screen; and if you press and hold it while it is on, the Voice Control screen appears. You can configure the Home button to perform other useful duties when you double-tap.

Customize the Home Button

1 Tap **General** in the Settings menu.

The General screen appears.

2 Tap **Home**.

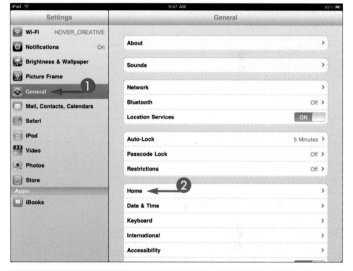

The Home screen appears.

3 Tap the screen you want to appear when you double-tap the Home button (■).

Note: Your choices are Home, Search, and iPod.

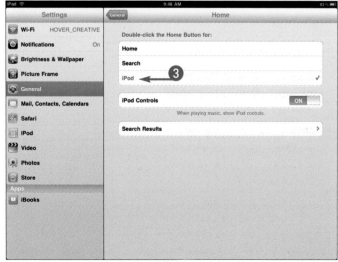

Adjust the Brightness of the Screen

Your iPad is equipped with sensors that enable it to automatically adjust the brightness of the screen according to ambient light. This feature is called Auto-Brightness. If the ambient light is dim, iPad automatically brightens the screen. If the ambient light is bright, the iPad screen dims. This is a hands-free way to find a balance between battery life and screen brightness. You can also manually adjust the screen brightness of your iPad to your own liking.

Adjust the Brightness of the Screen

① Tap **Brightness & Wallpaper**.

The **Brightness & Wallpaper** screen appears.

② Drag the **Brightness** slider to dim or brighten the screen.

Note: *Dragging the Brightness slider to the left dims the screen. Dragging the Brightness slider to the right brightens the screen.*

③ Tap the **Auto-Brightness** setting to the **Off** position.

iPad saves your new brightness settings.

Note: *If you do not turn off Auto-Brightness, iPad does not maintain your new brightness settings. It continues to adjust automatically when the ambient light changes.*

Turn Off Wi-Fi or Switch to Airplane Mode

When traveling on an airplane, you can place your iPad into Airplane mode, which disables any wireless features that may interfere with the operation of aircraft instruments. Airplane mode is a feature of the Wi-Fi + 3G model iPad only. While in Airplane mode and when the Wi-Fi has been deactivated, you can still enjoy downloaded content, such as music, videos, and eBooks.

Turn Off Wi-Fi or Switch to Airplane Mode

① Tap **Wi-Fi** in the Settings menu.

Note: *If you have the 3G iPad model, the actual Airplane mode setting is accessible on this screen.*

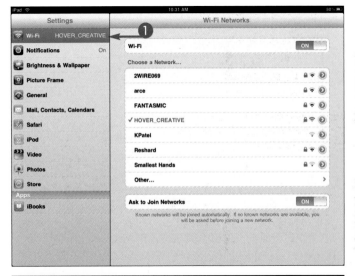

② Tap the **Wi-Fi** setting to the **Off** position.

Note: *For your 3G iPad, tap the Airplane Mode setting to the On position.*

Your iPad's wireless capabilities have been deactivated.

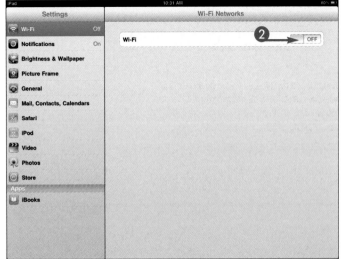

Change the iPad Wallpaper

Perhaps the most basic customization you can perform with your iPad is changing the default wallpaper for the Home screen. The iPad has several Apple-designed wallpapers from which to choose, but you can personalize your screen by choosing one of your own.

① Tap **Brightness & Wallpaper** in the Settings menu.

② Tap in the **Wallpaper** field.

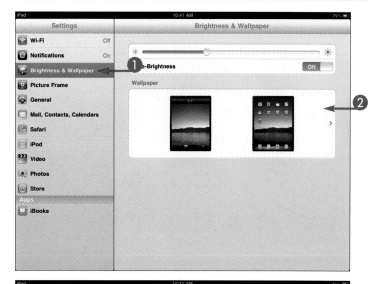

The photo collections on your iPad appear.

③ Tap the collection of photos from which you want to choose.

Note: At this point, by tapping **Wallpaper**, you can choose pre-existing wallpaper designed by Apple or you can choose one of your own photos.

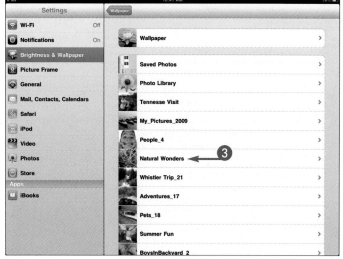

4 Tap the image you want to use.

The Move and Scale screen appears.

5 Position the image with your finger until it is situated the way you want it to appear.

The photo is repositioned.

Note: You can pinch and open your fingers to enlarge or decrease the scale of the image.

The scale of the photo is adjusted.

6 Tap **Set Both**.

The image is set as the wallpaper for both the Lock screen and the Home screen.

Note: Next to the Set Both button, you can choose to make the picture you have picked as the wallpaper for either the Lock screen or the Home screen. You can use a different image for each if you like.

How do I get my own photographs onto my iPad?

You can connect your iPad to your computer and sync the photographs that you have in iPhoto or Photoshop Elements to your iPad or you can use the iPad camera connection kit. The camera connection kit provides you with two ways of getting your photos onto your iPad. You can either attach your camera to the iPad with a USB cable or insert a memory card directly into the connector to transfer your photos. The camera connection kit is sold separately.

Configure Parental Controls

If children have access to your iPad or if they have one of their own, the iPad has parental control features that can help you restrict the content to which they are exposed on the web. You can restrict their access to popular online communities, such as YouTube, and even restrict downloading from the App Store and iTunes.

① Tap **General** in the Settings menu.

The General screen appears.

② Tap **Restrictions**.

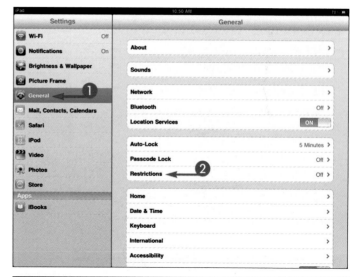

The Restrictions screen appears.

③ Tap **Enable Restrictions**.

iPad displays the Set Passcode screen so you can specify a four-digit code to use to override the parental controls.

Note: *This passcode is not the same passcode used to password-protect access to your iPad.*

④ Type the four-digit restriction passcode.

iPad prompts you to type the passcode again.

⑤ Type the four-digit restriction passcode again.

iPad returns you to the Restrictions screen and enables all controls.

⑥ Tap each setting to **On** or **Off** to enable or disable restrictions.

The restrictions are enabled.

Note: *You can tap the **In-App Purchases** setting to **Off** if you want to restrict children from making purchases within apps, such as iTunes.*

Note: *The **Ratings For** setting lets you set restrictions by using a specified country's rating system for Music, Podcasts, Movies, TV Shows, and Apps. For example, the rating PG applies to movies in the United States.*

Note: *You can tap a category, such as Music & Podcasts, Movies, TV Shows, and Apps, and then choose the highest rating you will allow for your children.*

⑦ Tap **General** to return to the General settings screen.

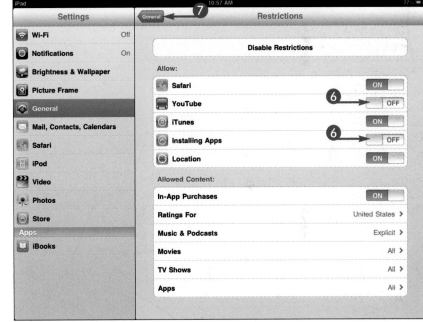

 TIPS

Can I turn off the restrictions?

Yes. But it requires that you know your passcode. Follow these steps:

① Tap **Settings** on the Home screen.

② Tap **General**.

③ Tap **Restrictions**.

④ Type the passcode.

⑤ Tap **Disable Restrictions**.

⑥ Type the passcode.

> Disable Restrictions

What if I forget my passcode?

You will have to connect your iPad to your computer and then restore your iPad software from iTunes.

Reset
the iPad

Over time and after many different configurations, you may want to clear all or some of your iPad's settings and then return the iPad to the default settings. You can choose from several different reset options. Resetting your iPad can give you a fresh start at configuring your iPad.

① Tap **Settings** on the Home screen.

The Settings screen appears.

② Tap **General**.

The General screen appears.

③ Tap **Reset**.

The Reset screen appears.

④ Tap the Reset option you want.

A dialog box appears, notifying you that all settings will be reset.

⑤ Tap **Reset**.

The settings you have specified are reset.

TIP

What does each of the reset options do?
The reset options available are as follows:

- **Reset All Settings:** Custom settings revert back to the factory default settings.
- **Erase All Content and Settings:** Custom settings are reset, and all data on your iPad is removed. You should use this option before gifting or selling your iPad.
- **Reset Network Settings:** Wi-Fi network settings are deleted.
- **Reset Keyboard Dictionary:** A list of all the keyboard recommendations you have rejected are cleared.
- **Reset Homescreen Layout:** This returns the Home screen icons to their default arrangements.
- **Reset Location Warnings:** This clears location preferences for your apps.

Cutting, Copying, and Pasting Editable and Non-Editable Text

Your iPad makes it easy for you to transfer data such as editable and non-editable text by copying or cutting it and pasting it in a new location. This feature comes in handy if you should ever find a block of text on a webpage that you would like to share with friends or family. You can copy the paragraph and then paste it into an email message. The procedure differs depending on if the text is editable or non-editable.

Cutting, Copying, and Pasting Text

Select and Copy Non-Editable Text

***Note:** An example of non-editable text would be text found on a website.*

1 Tap and hold in the section of the non-editable text that you want to copy.

A selection box with handles appears around the text. A button allowing you to Copy the text also appears.

2 Drag the handles of the selection box around the text that you want.

3 Tap **Copy**.

The text is placed on the Clipboard, which you do not see, but it is there.

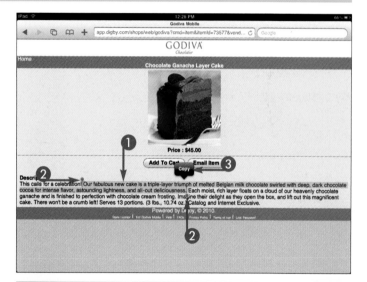

Select and Copy Editable Text

***Note:** An example of editable text would be a URL for a website or the body of an email message.*

1 Tap and hold until you see the magnifying glass and then release.

Two buttons appear, providing you with options.

2 Tap one of the options.

***Note:** Tap **Select** if you want to select only part of the text or tap **Select All** to select all the text.*

***Note:** In this example, Select was chosen.*

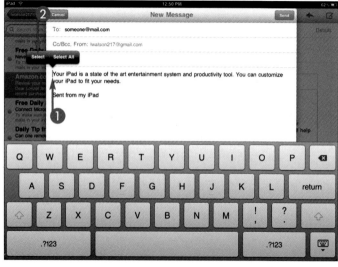

Part of the text is highlighted in blue and two more options appear, asking what you want to do with the text.

③ Tap and drag the selection handles around the text that you want.

④ Tap the option you want.

Note: Copy was chosen for this example.

⑤ Open the app in which you want to paste the text.

Note: In this example, I pasted into a new email message.

⑥ Tap where you want to paste the text.

⑦ Tap **Paste**.

iPad adds the copied text to the email.

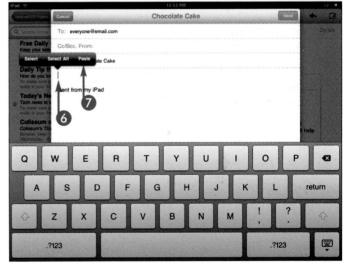

Can I undo a paste?
Yes. Sometimes, you find that you have copied the wrong data or maybe pasted it into the wrong area. You can undo the paste operation by shaking your iPad in your hands. The iPad motion sensor technology alerts the iPad that you want to undo the paste. A dialog box opens, prompting you to make a choice: Undo Paste or Cancel. Tap **Undo Paste** to reverse your most recent paste.

Copy and Paste a Photo

Your iPad makes it easy for you to copy and paste photos to a new location. The ability to copy and paste photos enables you to copy an image from your personal website and then paste it into another document or app, such as Mail. The process is very similar to copying and pasting non-editable text.

Copy and Paste a Photo

① Tap and hold the image you want to copy.

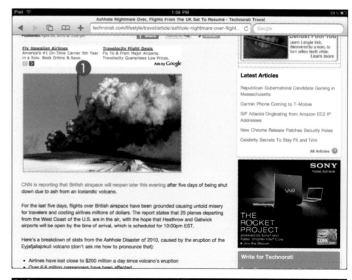

A pop-up menu of image options appears.

② Tap **Copy**.

The photo is copied into your iPad's memory.

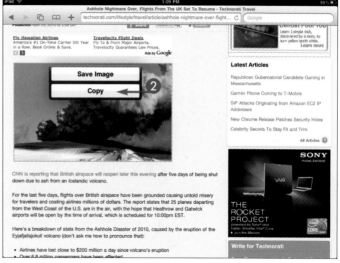

③ Open the app into which you want to paste the photo.

Note: *This example pastes the photo into an email message.*

④ Tap where you want the image to appear.

Options appear, asking you what you want to do.

⑤ Tap **Paste**.

iPad pastes the photo.

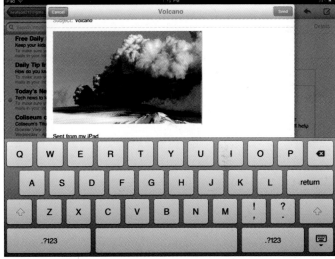

 TIP

Can I undo a paste?
Yes. Sometimes, you find that you have copied and pasted the wrong image or pasted it into the wrong area. You can undo the paste operation by shaking your iPad in your hands. The iPad motion sensor technology alerts the iPad that you want to reverse the paste. A dialog box opens, prompting you to make a choice: Undo Paste or Cancel. Tap **Undo Paste** to reverse your most recent paste.

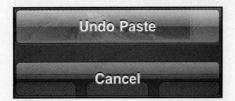

Search Your iPad by Using Spotlight

Spotlight is a simple search box that enables you to search your entire iPad for content. Although the iPad does not have a large hard drive like a computer, it is still capable of amassing plenty of content. Spotlight is a helpful tool for you to find content for which you do not know the exact location.

Search Your iPad by Using Spotlight

1 Tap the **Home** button (■) to return to the Home screen.

2 Tap ■ again to display the Spotlight screen.

Note: From the Home screen, you could have also flicked to the right to access the Spotlight screen.

③ Type the search text.

Items that match your search begin to appear on-screen.

④ Tap **Search**.

The complete search results appear.

⑤ Tap the item you were looking for.

The item opens.

Where exactly can you search with Spotlight?

Spotlight searches your entire iPad, including apps. Spotlight has the ability to search many apps on your iPad, including Mail, Contacts, Notes, iPod, and Calendar. You can use the Search field to search an individual app installed on your iPad or all of them simultaneously. Tap any of the app icons that appear in your search to open the app.

Getting the Most from the Internet

Your iPad offers many great features for experiencing all that the Internet has to offer. The Safari web browser provides you with many options for optimizing your web-browsing experience. In this chapter, you learn the basics of Internet access, Wi-Fi networks, and 3G service. You also learn how to customize the Safari security options as well as explore touch-screen navigation tips.

Understand Internet Access 60

Connect to a Wi-Fi Network
    for the First Time 62

Activate Your 3G Service 64

Change the Default Search Engine 66

Manage Multiple Web Browsers 68

Explore Web Browser Security and
    Privacy Options 70

Bookmark Your Favorite Websites 72

Explore Touch-Screen Navigation Tips 74

Turn On AutoFill 76

View an RSS Feed 78

Understand Internet Access

Before you can begin to enjoy the Internet on your iPad, you need to explore some basic information about Internet access. Understanding the role of an Internet Service Provider (ISP) and how to connect your iPad to the Internet for the first time can help get you online. Understanding the basics of Wi-Fi and 3G service can help you get the most from your iPad.

Understanding Internet Service Providers

An Internet Service Provider (ISP) is essentially the company that offers you and other customers like you access to the Internet through broadband or dialup access. Typically, for a monthly fee, the service provider supplies you with a software package, username and password, and hardware, such as a modem, enabling you to browse the World Wide Web. Along with providing Internet access, ISPs often offer website hosting and supply you with an email address which you can send and receive email. You will need an ISP before you can access the Internet with your iPad.

Understanding Wi-Fi

Wi-Fi is short for "wireless fidelity" and is often referred to as AirPort by Apple and even 802.11 by techies. Essentially, Wi-Fi is a wireless connection that uses radio waves that enable you to access the Internet remotely in your home, office, or classroom. The range for these wireless networks, also referred to as Wi-Fi hotspots, is usually 115 feet. Some public networks boost their signal to extend their range. You will need a wireless router connected to a host computer with Internet access to set up your own Wi-Fi network for your iPad. Consider protecting your Wi-Fi network with a password so other users cannot access your service.

Understanding 3G

3G is short for "third generation." The iPad Wi-Fi + 3G model is capable of accessing the Internet via 2G and 3G cellular networks as well as Wi-Fi hotspots. As long as your iPad is within a 3G coverage area, you can access the Internet from anywhere — even a moving vehicle. 3G cellular coverage is widespread throughout many countries, so you will not find yourself out of range very often. You need to sign up for a cellular data plan before you can join a cellular network with your iPad. You can check your carrier's availability in your area before you sign up.

Robo Wireless 3G Coverage

Understanding EDGE Cellular Technology

EDGE is short for Enhanced Data rates for GSM (Global System for Mobile Communication) Evolution and is part of your cellular data coverage. Downloads over an EDGE connection are much slower than downloads over a 3G cellular network. The advantage of EDGE is that it is even more widespread than 3G coverage. If you happen to be in an area where Wi-Fi hotspots and 3G coverage are unavailable, your iPad Wi-Fi + 3G model drops to EDGE mode to acquire a signal.

Connect to a Wi-Fi Network for the First Time

When you first fire up your iPad and attempt to access the Internet via Safari, Mail, YouTube, and so on, iPad searches for available Wi-Fi networks in range. The names of the networks that have been located appear in a list, and you are prompted to pick a Wi-Fi network. Understanding how to connect to a Wi-Fi network enables you to take advantage of the many things you can do on the Internet with your iPad.

Connect to a Wi-Fi Network for the First Time

1 Attempt to access the Internet for the first time.

Note: *You can attempt to access the Internet by tapping the* **Safari***,* **YouTube***, or* **Mail** *apps on the Home screen.*

iPad searches for available networks and provides a list of available networks.

2 Tap the network you want to use.

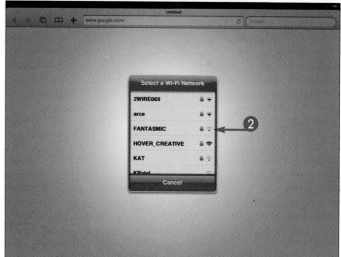

The on-screen keyboard appears.

Note: If the network is password-protected, iPad prompts you to type the password. If the network is not password-protected, iPad connects to the network.

3 Type the password by using the on-screen keyboard.

4 Tap **Join**.

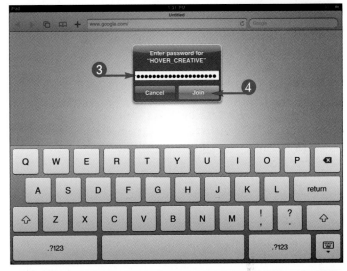

iPad connects to the network, a network signal icon (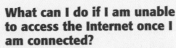) appears on the status bar, and the default web browser opens.

Note: The more bars that show in the 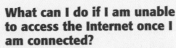, the stronger the signal.

 TIPS

What can I do if I am unable to join a Wi-Fi network?

Verify that you are choosing the correct Wi-Fi network. If the network is protected with a password, make sure that you typed the correct password. If you still cannot connect to the Wi-Fi network, you can try restarting the device and/or resetting the network setting under Settings on the Home screen. If you have a Wi-Fi + 3G model, consider turning off Wi-Fi and using a cellular connection instead.

What can I do if I am unable to access the Internet once I am connected?

A number of things could be the reason. The signal may be weak; you can determine this by looking at the  in the top-left corner of the iPad screen. Try moving closer to the hotspot. If the area that you are in has more than one Wi-Fi signal, confirm that you are using the correct network. If you are at home and using a Wi-Fi router, you can try turning it off and then turning it on again. You may need to refer to the router's documentation to reset the router.

Activate Your 3G Service

If you own the iPad Wi-Fi + 3G model, you can activate and cancel your service directly on the device. Your iPad also includes a metering system that lets you track how much data you have used during the service month. Learning how to activate your 3G service on your iPad enables you to take advantage of a cellular network for wireless Internet access.

Signing Up

You do not need to visit AT&T or the Apple Store to sign up for 3G service. You can sign up for a 3G data service plan right from your iPad by tapping Settings on the Home screen and then choosing Cellular Data. All you need to do is type your user information, choose a plan, and then type your credit card information to activate the service. As of this writing, AT&T does not require a contract for 3G service on the iPad Wi-Fi + 3G model.

Monitoring Data Usage

Your iPad also gives you the convenience of monitoring your data usage for your monthly plan under Settings. iPad also issues three alerts when you are about to reach your data limit: at 20%, 10%, and 0%. iPad also prompts you to add more data to your plan or wait until later with each alert. This makes it easier for you to conserve data if you are approaching your limit for that given month. If you choose Now, the Cellular Data Plan window opens, enabling you to update your data plan.

Managing Your Data Plan

You do not have to wait for an alert in order to update your 3G service plan. The iPad makes it easy for you to manage your data plan by giving you the option of adding another 250MB or the ability to upgrade to the Unlimited Data plan whenever you like. Because AT&T does not require that you sign a contract for 3G service — as of this writing — you sign up in monthly increments. You can also cancel your service and then sign up again when you need 3G service.

Understanding Roaming Charges

If you happen to find yourself in an area where AT&T does not have 3G coverage, you can use a cellular data network provided by another carrier. To use a different network, you can turn on Cellular Data Roaming by tapping Settings on the Home screen and then choosing **Cellular Data** to turn on Cellular Data Roaming. An important thing to keep in mind is that roaming charges can be quite costly. Make sure that you turn off roaming whenever it is not needed.

Change the Default Search Engine

When you tap the Safari app on the Home screen, your iPad immediately takes you to the default search engine — Google — from which you can begin your search. If you are more of a Yahoo person, your iPad makes it easy for you to designate Yahoo as the default search engine that opens when you tap Safari. Learning to change the default search engine helps you personalize your iPad.

Change the Default Search Engine

① Tap **Settings** on the Home screen.

The Settings screen appears.

② Tap **Safari**.

The Safari options appear.

③ Tap **Search Engine**.

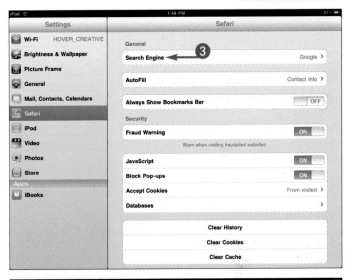

The Search Engine screen appears.

Note: The current default search screen has a check mark next to it.

④ Tap **Yahoo!**.

● iPad places a check mark next to the Yahoo! option and makes Yahoo your default search engine.

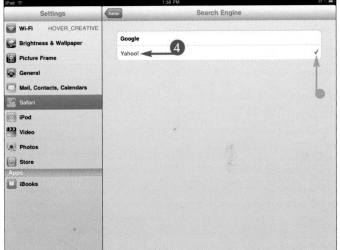

Is there any way that I can set my default webpage to a site other than Google or Yahoo?

No. Unlike your computer, you cannot set the default webpage to whatever you like — for example, your favorite online news source. Your only choices are Google and Yahoo. With that being said, Safari opens to whatever page you had visited last. Before you leave Safari, you could make sure you return to the page you would like it to open to. It is not an automatic fix, but at least Safari opens with the page you want.

Google

Yahoo!

Manage Multiple Web Browsers

Your iPad makes it easy for you to open multiple web browser screens at the same time, load different pages into them, and navigate between the multiple pages. You can view multiple open pages in a grid, enabling you to move quickly between pages with just the tap of your fingers. The ability to manage multiple browser pages enables you to perform multiple searches.

Manage Multiple Web Browsers

① Tap **Safari** on the Home screen.

Safari opens.

② Tap the **Pages** icon ( ) on the menu bar.

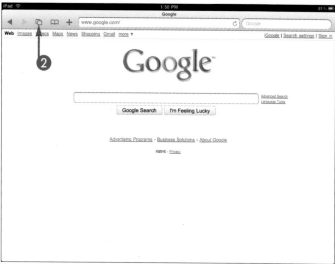

Safari displays a new blank page, along with the current page as a thumbnail.

③ Tap **New Page**.

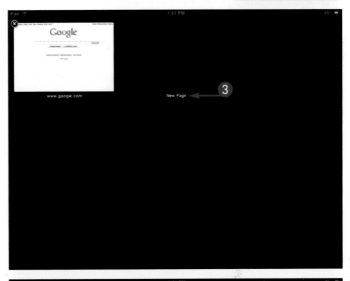

The new page opens full screen, along with the on-screen keyboard. A blinking cursor appears in the Search field.

④ Load a new website.

Note: You can do this by typing a web address, typing a search, or even tapping a bookmark.

⑤ Repeat steps **1** to **4** for additional pages if needed.

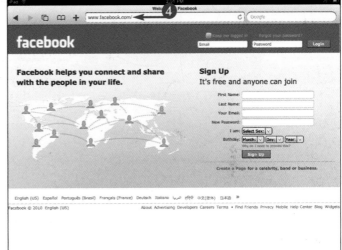

 TIP

Any tips on navigating between multiple pages?

Yes. Your iPad can have up to nine webpages open at the same time. You can tap the **Pages** icon (▢) on the menu bar to see all the pages at once in thumbnails. You can navigate between the pages you have open in this view, and you can also tap the ⊗ located in the upper-left corner of the webpage thumbnail in order to delete pages you no longer need.

Explore Web Browser Security and Privacy Options

When you surf the Internet, you can open your iPad up to security risks that can compromise your privacy. Learning about browser security options can help you protect your iPad from security risks on the Internet. The security options for your iPad are located in Safari under Settings.

Exploring Fraud Warning

Fraudulent websites designed to appear as legitimate companies can pose real threats to your privacy. The hook that many of these frauds use is to send you an email that requests you to update your account information on their site. The email can appear from a reputable company of which you may actually have an account, such as eBay. The scheme is to get you to hand over your personal information. Once it has your information, it is easy for an experienced criminal to steal your identity. You should turn on Fraud Warning so Safari can warn you about the suspect page and not load the website.

Understanding JavaScript

JavaScript is a scripting language that exists within the HTML for a webpage and is used for such things as rollovers. JavaScript can also be used for foul purposes by those who are inclined to do so. By default, your iPad is set to support JavaScript. You can turn JavaScript support off if you choose to visit a suspect website. Keep in mind that most webpages do not work without JavaScript, so you should not turn it off permanently.

Understanding Pop-Up Blocking

Pop-up ads are a form of aggressive online advertising, often used to attract traffic to a certain site. Pop-ups get their name from their actions. A site that you are viewing may open a new web browser page and load an advertisement into it, which can be annoying. By default, your iPad is configured to block pop-ups. It is important to note here that pop-ups can serve legitimate purposes, such as login pages, media players, and announcements. When navigating certain websites, you may need to set the Block Pop-ups option to Off.

Exploring Cookies

Cookies are small text files that some websites store on your iPad to track your website activity. One common use of them is for online shopping sites to record your personal information and track your shopping cart. On the more annoying end, when you visit some websites, the server can store one of these text files on your computer as a means to track your movements and display advertisements personalized for your viewing habits. By default, your iPad is set to accept cookies only from sites that you visit and rejects all third-party cookies. You can also configure your iPad to Never accept cookies or Always accept cookies. The default option of From visited is the better option of these three.

Clearing the Browser History and the Cache

Behind the scenes, Safari secretly records the places you have visited on the web, known as History. History is a great feature if you need to retrace your steps to find a website for which you may have forgotten the name. The contents of the pages you have visited are stored in what is called the browser cache. The information stored in the browser cache enables websites to load faster when you visit them. Your iPad gives you the ability to clear the History of the webpages you have visited. You can also clear the cache to try to solve loading issues that may occur.

Bookmark Your Favorite Websites

When you are surfing the Internet, your iPad makes it easy for you to save your favorite websites as bookmarks. Adding a bookmark for a website enables you to skip the process of typing in a web address to revisit the page. Bookmarked webpages appear in a list, and all you have to do is tap the bookmark to visit the page.

Bookmark Your Favorite Websites

① Navigate to the website that you want to save.

Note: *You can do this by typing the web address or typing in the Search field and tapping and choosing an option from the search list.*

② Tap the **Plus** icon (+) on the address bar.

A menu appears, presenting you with three options for the website.

③ Tap **Add Bookmark**.

A blinking cursor appears in the address field.

4 Type a new name for the page if needed.

● The address for the website appears beneath the name field.

5 Tap **Save**.

By default, your iPad saves the website at the top level of the Bookmarks list.

TIPS

Can I sync bookmarks on my computer with my iPad?

Yes. If you have a Mac or a PC, you can sync the bookmarks with the Safari web browser on your Mac and the Internet Explorer or Safari browser on your PC with your iPad. You can also sync bookmarks with MobileMe.

Can I edit the bookmarks on my iPad?

Yes. You can tap the **Bookmarks** icon () on the main menu bar and tap a bookmark or folder that contains the bookmark you want to edit. You can create new bookmark folders, delete bookmark folders, reposition a bookmark or folder by dragging, and edit the name of a bookmark or web address.

Explore Touch-Screen Navigation Tips

Your iPad places the power of the Internet and many entertainment and productive software apps at your fingertips — literally. If you are used to navigating websites and apps with your iPhone or iPod touch, then you are familiar with zooming, scrolling, and turning pages with your fingers. Understanding how to navigate by using the touch screen enables you to get the most from your iPad.

Scrolling and Zooming

Scrolling webpages and zooming into a specific area on a website are common practices. You can scroll up and down webpages with a flick of your finger — either up or down. To get a closer look at a graphic on a page — for example, merchandise in an online store — you can place your thumb and forefinger on the screen, pinch them closely, and then move them apart to zoom into an image. To zoom out of the image, place your two fingers apart on the screen and then pinch them closed. You do not have to be exact when returning the page to its previous scale. Just pinch your fingers closed, and iPad snaps the page back to the default scale.

One Tap

A single tap with one finger is perhaps the most used navigation method on the touch screen. You can tap a link to open a new webpage as well as tap in an online form to receive a blinking cursor and to make the on-screen keyboard appear so you can begin typing. If you are reading down a long webpage and want to return to the top of the page, you can tap on the menu bar area, and iPad returns you to the top of the page.

Double-Tapping

Double-tapping is a quick way to zoom into pages. For example, if you are reading text, a chart, or a table that is particularly small, you can double-tap to magnify the page. To magnify a specific area of the page, just double-tap on top of that specific area to magnify it. To return the page to its original scale, just double-tap the page again.

Tapping, Holding, and Dragging

Tapping and then holding and dragging can perform some very helpful functions on your iPad. On a Mac computer, you can hover the mouse cursor over a link on a webpage to view the URL where the link will send you. You can do the same on your iPad by tapping and holding your finger on a link. You also receive a menu that gives you the options to Open, Open in New Page, and Copy. Tapping and holding on text highlights the text and gives you the option of copying the text. iPad highlights the area you want to copy in blue. You can drag the selection to encompass more text. If you tap in the white area between two paragraphs, your iPad highlights the entire body of text and gives you the option of copying it.

Viewing in Landscape

The iPad also enables you to view websites and apps in various ways according to how you hold the iPad. For example, when using email, you hold the iPad in landscape orientation so you can view your email as a split screen, displaying both open email and messages in your Inbox. You can view an open email by itself by holding the iPad in the portrait orientation. The iPad contains internal sensors that use gravity to sense the orientation of the device; thus, if the iPad is laying flat on a table and you rotate it, the orientation does not change.

Considering a Larger Keyboard

The iPad's on-screen keyboard provides you with the comfort of typing with an almost standard-sized keyboard. If the on-screen keyboard does not suffice for your practical everyday use, you can consider investing in a full-sized keyboard. The iPad keyboard dock gives you the convenience of a full-sized keyboard while enabling your iPad to be charged at the same time. A Bluetooth keyboard provides you with the flexibility of using a full-sized keyboard with your iPad without a physical connection.

Turn On AutoFill

Occasionally, you may find yourself filling out a form on your iPad, which may require you to fill in multiple fields of information, such as first and last name, mailing address, email address, and so on. You can turn on AutoFill to help you fill out these forms faster by having your iPad automatically fill fields with information found in your Contacts list.

Turn On AutoFill

① Tap **Settings** on the Home screen.

The Settings screen appears.

② Tap **Safari**.

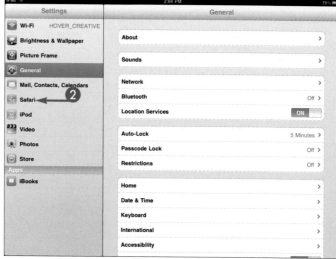

The Safari options appear.

③ Tap **AutoFill**.

The AutoFill screen appears.

④ Tap **Use Contact Info** to the **On** position.

The My Info field is now active.

⑤ Tap the **My Info** field.

A list of contacts located in your All Contacts list appears.

⑥ Tap the contact whose information you want iPad to use for autofill.

Note: This step requires that you have your own personal contact information in your All Contacts list.

The All Contacts list closes, and your iPad uses the information listed in the contact to automatically fill out forms.

How can I use the Names and Passwords option?

You can tap the Names and Passwords option to the On position so Safari remembers the names and passwords you have used on sites you have visited. When you return to these webpages, Safari automatically fills in this information in the proper fields for you. Be careful when using this feature, especially if more than one person uses your iPad. With Names and Passwords left On, it will be easy for someone to access your personal information when you supply that person with your password.

View an RSS Feed

Real Simple Syndication (RSS) feeds are special files that contain the most recent updated works on a website. If your favorite blog does not post new content frequently but does so on an irregular basis, RSS feeds are a great way to receive the most recent posts displayed in your Safari web browser for your convenience. Not all blogs have RSS feeds.

View an RSS Feed

1 Tap **Safari** on the Home screen.

Safari opens.

2 Navigate to a site that you know has an RSS feed.

The site opens.

3 Locate the link to the RSS feed and then tap it.

Note: Look for an RSS icon () or a link that says View Feed XML.

4 Tap the link to the RSS feed.

The web-based RSS reader opens the feed.

Note: The most current posts are listed, of which you can tap and read the most recent articles.

TIP

What is an efficient way to access my RSS feeds?
A great way to access your RSS feeds is to bookmark them like you would any other site. Follow the steps in the section "Bookmark Your Favorite Websites" to bookmark your RSS feeds.

CHAPTER 5

Maximizing Email on the iPad

You can use your iPad's Mail app to send email and read email from friends, family, and colleagues. Your iPad makes it very easy for you to check email when you are on the go, supplying you with many of the same mail features you enjoy on your Mac or Windows computer. In this chapter, you learn how to set up an email account on your iPad as well as how to manage multiple email accounts and features.

Learn about Managing Email Accounts 82

Add an Email Account for the First Time 84

Create a New Email Account 86

Specify the Default Email Account................88

Switch to Another Email Account..................90

Disable an Email Account................................92

Use a Different Server Port 94

Configure Authentication for
    Outgoing Mail...96

Automatically Check for New Emails............98

Email a Link to a Webpage 100

Set Message Font Size....................................102

Create a Custom iPad Signature 104

Disable Remote Message Images................106

Learn about Managing Email Accounts

Understand the Mail App

The Mail app on your iPad is a scaled down but very capable version of the email program you enjoy on the Mac OS X and Windows operating systems. The Mail app has been optimized for your iPad, providing you with features and settings that make it very convenient to use while you travel. You can configure your email to access accounts already set on your computer and even create accounts on the iPad itself.

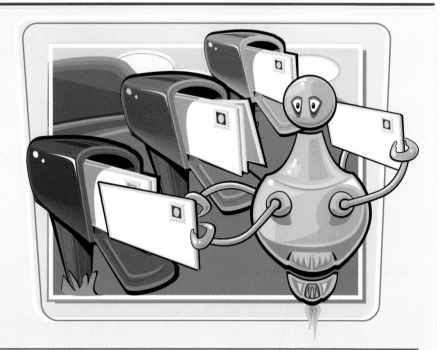

Connect with Email Services

Out of the box, the iPad recognizes five email services: Microsoft Exchange, MobileMe, Google Gmail, Yahoo Mail, and AOL. All you need to set up one of these accounts is the address and the account password. One of the most effective ways to use email on your iPad is to set up the Mail app to use an email account that you already use on your home computer. Syncing your iPad with your home computer enables you to check your email while traveling.

Set Up an iPad-Only Account

You can also set up an account that is different from the five email services your iPad recognizes. Your iPad also supports various email protocols, such as POP (Post Office Protocol) and IMAP (Internet Message Access Protocol). If you want to configure one of these protocols, you can ask your network administrator or email service provider what type of email account you currently have. This option takes considerably more work on your part, as opposed to simply syncing your Gmail or Yahoo account.

Specify the Default Email Account

Your iPad is capable of accessing multiple email accounts. You can specify which email account the Mail app opens when you tap the Mail app on the Home screen. If you have a primary email account to where most of your important messages are sent, you can set this account as your default email for quick access.

Switch, Disable, and Delete Accounts

After you have specified an email account as the default, you can easily switch it to another account if needed. You can conserve your iPad's battery life by checking fewer email accounts. You can achieve this by temporarily disabling an account or by deleting an account. If one of your email accounts has become less relevant, you should consider deleting that account.

Add an Email Account for the First Time

One way to access email on your iPad is to set up the Mail app to connect to an email account that is already set up on your home computer. The iPad recognizes five email services with a minimal amount of interaction on your behalf: Microsoft Exchange, MobileMe, Google Gmail, Yahoo Mail, and AOL. Adding an email account enables you to check your most important email accounts while on the road.

Add an Email Account for the First Time

① Tap **Mail** on the Home screen.

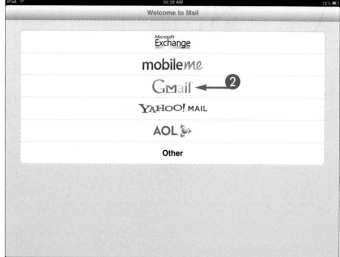

The Add Account screen appears.

② Tap the name of the email service you are adding.

The Add Account screen appears.

Note: This example uses Gmail.

③ Tap the **Name** field and then type your name.

Note: This is the name shown when you exchange emails.

④ Tap the **Address** field and then type the address for the existing account.

⑤ Tap the **Password** field and then type the password for the existing account.

⑥ Tap the **Description** field and then type what kind of email account you are adding.

⑦ Tap **Save**.

The Verifying email account information screen appears.

If the information you provided was correct, your email account has now been set up.

TIP

How do I add another email account after I have set up the first one?
You can add a second email account by following these steps:

① Tap **Settings** on the Home screen.

② Tap **Mail, Contacts, Calendars**.

Your iPad displays the Mail, Contacts, Calendars screen.

③ Tap **Add Account** to access the Add Account screen.

④ Follow steps **2** to **7** to set up one of the five email services your iPad recognizes.

_____@gmail.com	>
Mail	
Add Account...	>

Create a New Email Account

You may find it necessary to create an email account that exists only on your iPad — perhaps for an iPad mailing list. Your iPad Mail app supports both the Post Office Protocol (POP) and Internet Message Access Protocol (IMAP) email account types. These types of accounts are what you receive through your ISP, such as Comcast or RoadRunner. You will need specific information for the new account, including the host name of the incoming and outgoing mail servers, to create a new email account on your iPad.

Create a New Email Account

① Tap **Mail, Contacts, Calendars** in the Settings menu.

Your iPad displays the Mail, Contacts, Calendars screen.

② Tap **Add Mail Account**.

The Add Mail Account screen appears.

③ Tap **Other**.

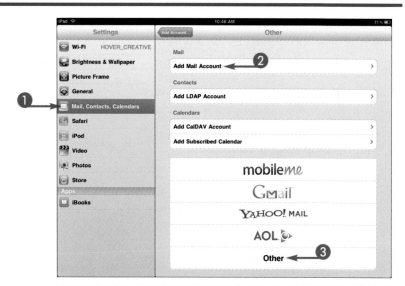

④ Tap **Add Mail Account**.

The New Account screen appears.

⑤ Tap the fields and then type the appropriate data into the **Name**, **Address**, **Password**, and **Description** fields.

⑥ Tap **Save**.

7 Tap the account type for the new email.

8 Type the host name, username, and password into the **Incoming Mail Server** section.

9 Type the host name, username, and password into the **Outgoing Mail Server** section.

Note: If your service provider requires a username and password, type those too.

10 Tap **Save**.

Your iPad verifies the account information and then returns you to the Mail Settings screen. The new account is added to the Accounts list.

Which is the most popular account type?

POP is the most common. Incoming messages for an email account are temporarily stored on the provider's mail server. Typically, when you connect to the POP server, the email downloads to your device and is then removed from the server. By default, your iPad actually saves a copy on the server. IMAP works with your email messages only on the server. You will need to manage the contents of the server so you do not fill your storage quota. Once you fill your quota, you will no longer be able to receive new mail until space has been freed.

What are the benefits of having your email stored only on the server?

When your email is stored on the server, you have the benefit of accessing those emails from multiple devices.

Specify the Default Email Account

Once you have set up multiple email accounts, your iPad will specify one as the default. You can specify a different account as the default mail account for your iPad to open when you tap the Mail app on the Home screen. Specifying a default email gives you quick access to your primary email.

Specify the Default Email Account

① Tap **Settings** on the Home screen.

The Settings screen appears.

② Tap **Mail, Contacts, Calendars**.

Your iPad displays the Mail, Contacts, Calendars screen.

③ Scroll down the screen and then tap **Default Account**.

The Default Account Screen appears.

● The current default account is shown with a check mark next to it.

④ Tap the account that you want to use as the default.

A check mark appears next to the email account you tapped.

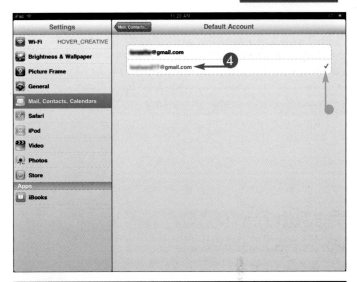

⑤ Tap the **Mail, Contacts, Calendars** button.

Your iPad returns to the Mail, Contacts, Calendars screen.

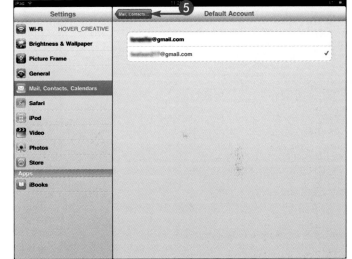

TIP

How does the Mail app choose the default email account once you have more than one?

The Mail app specifies the first email account that you created on the iPad as the default email account. When you create an email message from other iPad apps, such as Photos or Safari, or by tapping the email address in Contacts, it is sent by using the default email account.

Switch to Another Email Account

When you tap the Mail app on the Home screen, you are usually taken to the Inbox of the default email account. You can also switch from the current account to view the contents of the Inbox for your other iPad mail accounts. The ability to switch between accounts enables you to monitor the activities of multiple accounts.

Switch to Another Email Account

① Tap **Mail** on the Home screen.

Note: The Mail app opens to whatever screen you viewed last, so if you viewed the Inbox last, the app displays the contents of the Inbox.

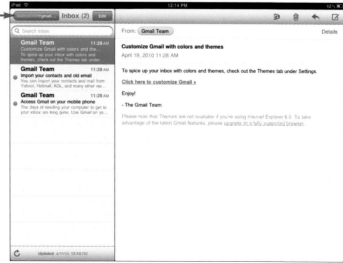

② Tap the **Mail Address** button.

③ Tap the **Accounts** button that appears in the top-left corner of the screen.

The Accounts screen displays all of your iPad's email accounts.

④ Tap the account you want to view.

Mail displays a list of the account's folders.

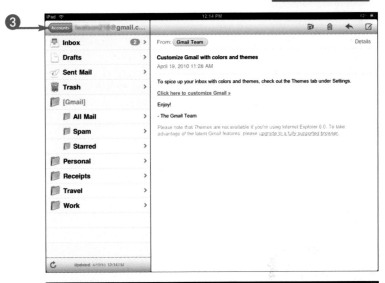

⑤ Repeat steps **2** to **4** to view the contents of another account's Inbox.

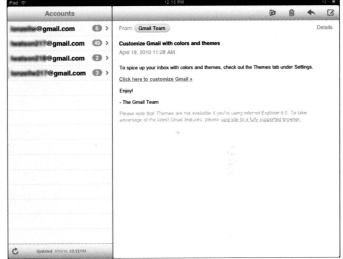

TIP

If I change the settings for one of my email accounts on my iPad, will it change the settings on my computer when I sync?

No. Your email account settings can only be synced from your computer to your iPad, not the other way around. This enables you to customize your email settings for an email account on your iPad without changing email account settings on your computer.

Disable an Email Account

The Mail app on the iPad continuously checks for new emails for the accounts you have created. This repeated checking for email can more or less drain your battery power. You can temporarily disable an email address to conserve more of your battery power.

Disable an Email Account

① Tap **Settings** on the Home screen.

The Settings screen appears.

② Tap **Mail, Contacts, Calendars**.

The Mail, Contacts, Calendars screen appears.

③ Tap the account you want to disable.

The account's settings appear.

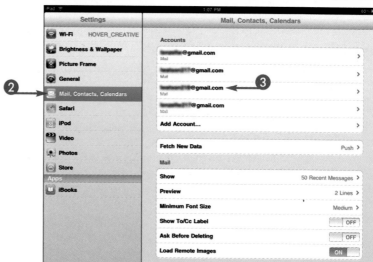

④ Tap the **Account** switch to **Off**.

The account has now been disabled.

⑤ Tap **Done**.

The email account is disabled.

TIP

Are there other ways I can save battery power other than disabling an email account?

There are many, but in regard to email, you can do a few things in particular. Accounts such as Microsoft Exchange, MobileMe, and Yahoo are referred to as push accounts. This means that when new messages are available, they are pushed/delivered to your iPad. This can eat your battery power, so consider turning off Push in the Mail settings. You can also check fewer email accounts by deleting an account.

Use a Different Server Port

If you are experiencing problems sending email from your POP account, try changing the outgoing server port to solve the issue. You can contact your ISP prior to specifying another port to make sure it is not blocking the port to which you want to switch.

Use a Different Server Port

① Tap **Settings** on the Home screen.

The Settings screen appears.

② Tap **Mail, Contacts, Calendars**.

The Mail, Contacts, Calendars screen appears.

③ Tap the POP account you want to edit.

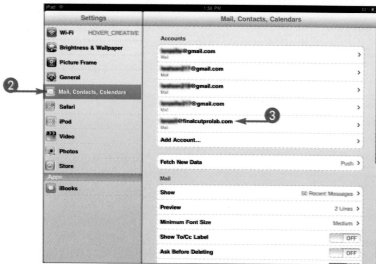

The account's settings appear.

④ Scroll down to the bottom of the screen and then tap **Advanced**.

The Advanced screen appears.

⑤ Tap **Server Port** in the Incoming Settings section.

The on-screen keyboard appears.

⑥ Type the port number.

What if I still experience outgoing email problems?

Check to see if all your settings are accurate. If you are still experiencing problems, call your ISP to verify if your account is set up correctly in the Mail app. Your ISP also can alert you to any policy conflicts that may be preventing you from sending email from a specific account.

Configure Authentication for Outgoing Mail

Authentication is a safety measure used to confirm that you are indeed the sender of the email and not a spammer. If your ISP requires authentication for outgoing mail, you can set up your email account to provide the appropriate credentials. The specification of a username and password is a common type of authentication.

Configure Authentication for Outgoing Mail

① Tap **Settings** on the Home screen.

The Settings screen appears.

② Tap **Mail, Contacts, Calendars**.

The Mail, Contacts, Calendars screen appears.

③ Tap the POP account you want to edit.

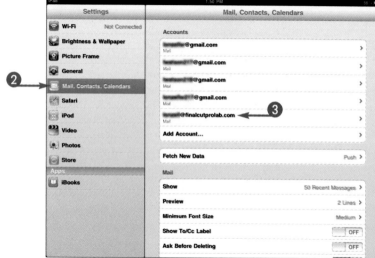

The account's settings appear.

4️⃣ Scroll down and then tap **SMTP**.

The SMTP screen appears.

5️⃣ Tap in the **Primary Server** field.

6️⃣ Tap **Authentication** in the Outgoing Mail Server section.

The Authentication screen appears.

7️⃣ Tap **Password**.

How many ISPs require authentication?

Many ISPs now require SMTP (Simple Mail Transfer Protocol) authentication for outgoing mail because of problems with junk email. You can check with your ISP to see if this applies to your service.

Automatically Check for New Emails

By default, the Mail app manually checks for new email messages whenever you tell it to. This is done by simply checking the Inbox for an account or by tapping the Refresh button ( ) on the left side of the menu bar. Occasionally, you may want your iPad to automatically check for emails. This feature can come in handy if you are preoccupied and waiting for an important email.

① Tap **Settings** on the Home screen.

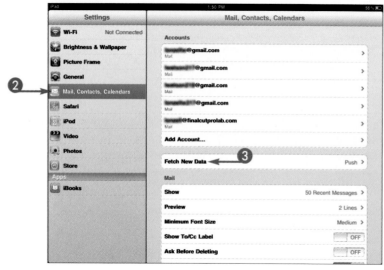

The Settings screen appears.

② Tap **Mail, Contacts, Calendars**.

The Mail, Contacts, Calendars screen appears.

③ Tap **Fetch New Data**.

The Fetch Data screen appears.

4 Tap the interval you want to use in the Fetch section.

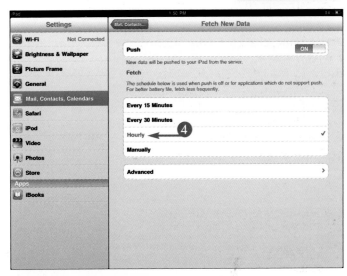

5 Tap the **Mail, Contacts, Calendar** button to return to the previous screen.

6 Repeat steps **1** to **4** to return to manually checking for new emails.

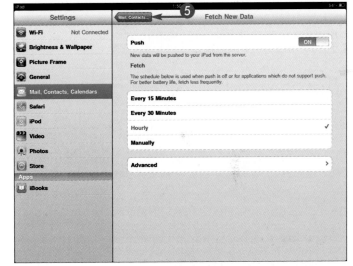

TIP

Should I keep my iPad set to automatically check mail?
To conserve battery power, you should consider returning your iPad back to manually checking for new messages. You could also configure your iPad to check for new emails less frequently by choosing **Every 30 minutes** or **Hourly**. If you find the use of battery life miniscule, by all means, continue to have your iPad check for messages at regular intervals.

Email a Link to a Webpage

Your iPad makes it easy for you to email a link to a cool website to friends, family, or colleagues. With just a few taps in the Safari app, you can share what you find with others.

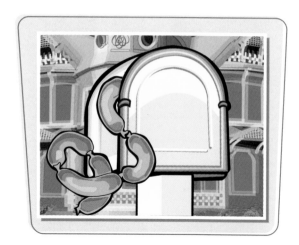

① Tap **Safari** on the Home screen.

The Safari app opens.

② Tap the **URL** field and then type the web address for the website you want to email.

Note: *You can also perform a search with the Search field to navigate to the site you want to email.*

③ Tap **Go**.

Safari takes you to the website.

Note: If you performed a search, the search results appear, from which you can tap to open the desired webpage.

④ Tap the **Plus** button (✚) on the menu bar.

A dialog box with several options opens.

⑤ Tap **Mail Link to this Page**.

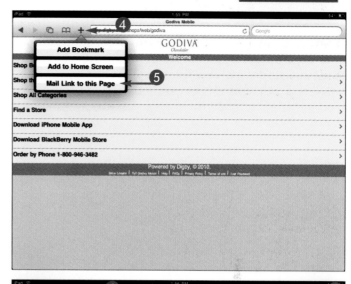

A new email message opens.

⑥ Type an email address or choose a recipient from your Contacts list.

Note: An email address must be listed for the contact if you choose someone from your Contacts list as a recipient.

Note: You can edit the message if you need to.

⑦ Tap **Send**.

The message is sent to the recipient.

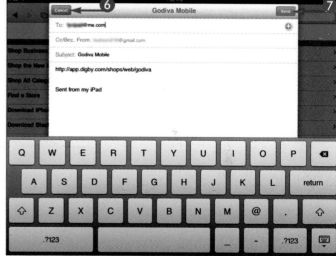

Are there other ways to email links to websites?

Yes. But some of them are not as streamlined as choosing the Mail Link to this Page option found in Safari. You can copy the URL of the webpage and then open the Mail app and paste the URL into a new message. Some websites are equipped with an option similar to the Mail Link to this Page option that can be found somewhere on the webpage. The mail option in Safari is a quick fix.

Your iPad makes it easy for you to change the font size for emails. You can set a minimum font size for emails, making them easier to read. If an email uses a larger font size than you specify, the font remains as is. If the font is smaller, your iPad scales up the font size accordingly.

Set Message Font Size

① Tap **Settings** on the Home screen.

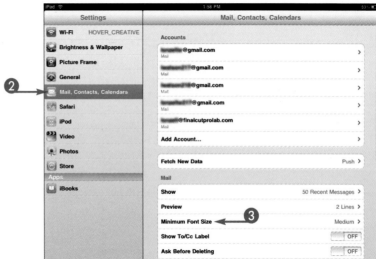

The Settings screen appears.

② Tap **Mail, Contacts, Calendars**.

The Mail, Contacts, Calendars screen appears.

③ Tap **Minimum Font Size**.

The Minimum Font Size screen appears.

④ Tap the minimum font size you want.

The Mail app now uses the minimum font size you have specified when displaying messages.

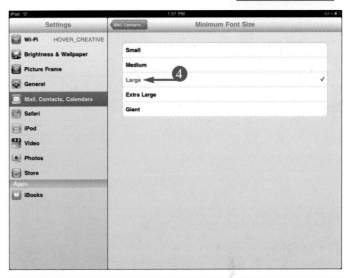

⑤ Tap the **Mail, Contacts, Calendars** button to return to the previous menu.

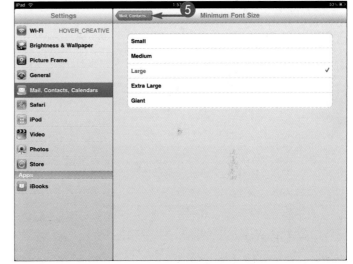

TIP

What can I do if I have trouble seeing an app on my iPad?

The iPad is equipped with a Zoom feature, which allows you to zoom into any app. You can use the Zoom feature to magnify the entire screen up to five times the normal size for increased readability. This feature works on the Home, Unlock, and Spotlight screens. You can also magnify apps that you purchase from the App Store. By default, the Zoom feature is disabled. To enable it, you will need to configure the triple-click function.

Create a Custom iPad Signature

The Mail app enables you to customize your own email signature, the same as you would in the default mail program on your Mac. Creating a custom signature enables you to add your own personal touch to the bottom of outgoing email messages in the form of a block of text displaying your contact information or a short quote.

① Tap **Settings** on the Home screen.

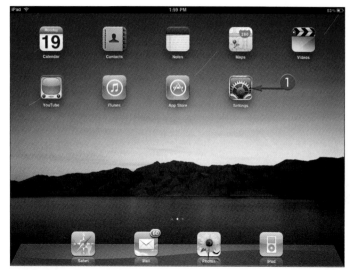

The Settings screen appears.

② Tap **Mail, Contacts, Calendars**.

The Mail, Contacts, Calendars screen appears.

③ Tap **Signature**.

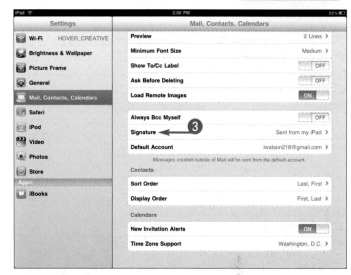

The Signature screen appears along with the on-screen keyboard.

④ Type the signature that you want to use.

Note: An email signature can be as short as one word, such as "Cheers," to a complete quote. Short is best.

⑤ Tap **Mail, Contacts, Calendars**.

The Mail app saves your signature and uses it for all outgoing email messages.

TIP

Can I return to the original signature?
The Mail app does not provide a way to cancel your edit and return to the original signature itself, but you can always write in "Sent from my iPad" yourself. Consider adding a personal line of your own and then place "Sent from my iPad" underneath it so the recipient knows the message originated from your iPad.

Disable Remote Message Images

You can disable images in the emails that you receive for faster load times and, more importantly, to help protect your privacy. If an image sent to you in an email is not attached to the actual email but kept on a remote server, your email will have to connect to the server to download the image. In the case of junk mail, this can open you up to "web bugs." Essentially, when you download the image from a remote server, the sender can find out personal information about you that could be used for marketing purposes.

Disable Remote Message Images

① Tap **Settings** on the Home screen.

The Settings screen appears.

② Tap **Mail, Contacts, Calendars**.

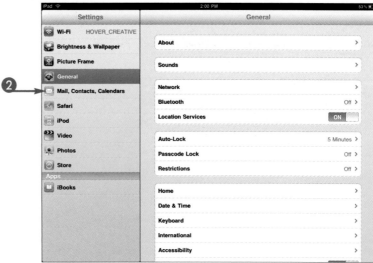

The Mail, Contacts, Calendars screen appears.

③ Scroll down and then tap the **Load Remote Images** switch to the **Off** position.

The setting is saved, and your iPad no longer displays remote images in your emails.

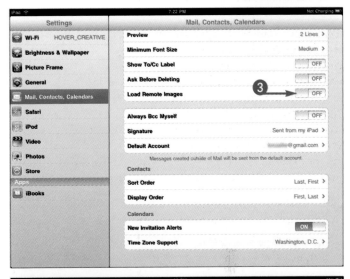

④ Press the Home button to return to the Home screen.

TIP

What exactly is a web bug?

A *web bug* is a reference embedded into HTML-formatted emails to images that reside on a remote server. When you open the email and image, Mail downloads the image by using an address for the remote server. In doing this, some marketers can learn information about you and track your surfing habits across the Internet. Websites can also contain web bugs.

CHAPTER

6

Syncing the iPad

Your iPad is a fully capable, stand-alone device, but you can also share much of the content that is on your computer with your iPad. Content found on your computer, such as apps downloaded from the App Store, iTunes music, movies, TV shows, calendar events, and contacts, are just some of the things you can share with your iPad. In this chapter, you learn how to connect your iPad to your computer and sync your fun — as well as productive — content with your iPad by using iTunes.

Connect Your iPad to a Computer...............110

Prevent Your iPad from Syncing
    Automatically................................112

Sync Your Contacts List...................114

Sync Your Calendar 116

Sync Your Email Account..................118

Sync Your Bookmarks.......................120

Sync Music and Music Videos 122

Sync Podcasts 124

Sync Audiobooks 126

Sync TV Show Episodes.....................128

Sync Photos on Your Computer
    with Your iPad...............................130

Save Photos from Emails..................132

Import Photos from Your Camera 134

Connect Your iPad to a Computer

Your iPad needs to be connected to your computer in order to share content. You can connect your iPad to your computer in a couple ways. Once you have connected your iPad to your Mac or PC, you can begin syncing/sharing content between your computer and your iPad.

Connect Your iPad to a Computer

① Turn on your computer.

② Take the USB to Dock connector and place the USB end into a USB port on your computer.

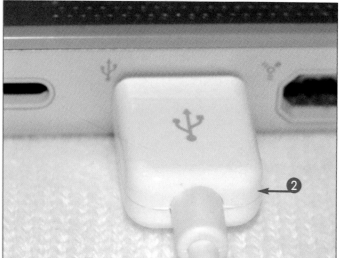

③ Turn on your iPad.

④ Attach the USB to Dock connector to your iPad.

Your iPad charges as it is connected to your computer.

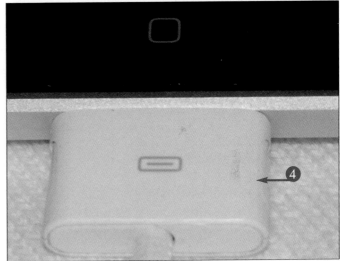

TIPS

Can I connect my iPad to the computer by using iPad accessories?

Yes. If you want to use the iPad dock or iPad keyboard dock while using your iPad, you can run the USB to Dock cable to your computer from either of these docks rather than directly from the iPad.

My iPad does not charge when connected to my computer. Why?

You should make sure that all cables are connected securely; if that does not work, you should try using another USB port. If you have your iPad connected to the USB port located on your keyboard, try moving it to a USB port located on the actual computer. The USB port located on the keyboard may not transfer enough power to charge the iPad.

Prevent Your iPad from Syncing Automatically

By default, when you connect your iPad to your computer and launch iTunes, contacts, calendars, and other data are automatically synced. This is fine if the content on your computer requires less storage capacity than what is available on your iPad and if you do not care to handpick what information is shared. As you acquire more iPad-friendly content on your computer, you will need to pick and choose what information you want to sync by performing a manual sync. First, you need to prevent your iPad from automatically syncing.

Perform a Manual Sync

① Launch iTunes on your computer.

The iTunes app opens on your computer.

② Click **iTunes** for a Mac or click **Edit** for a Windows computer.

③ Click **Preferences**.

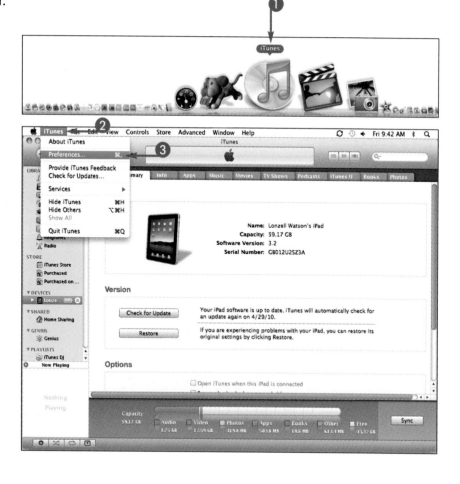

The iTunes preferences appear.

④ Click the **Devices** tab.

The Devices pane opens.

⑤ Click the **Prevent iPods, iPhones, and iPads from syncing automatically** check box (☐ changes to ☑).

⑥ Click **OK**.

The settings are saved.

Note: The iPad will now not automatically sync when you connect your iPad to your computer.

TIP

Is there any way that I can avoid automatic sync, one time, without deactivating it?

Yes. You can bypass the automatic sync on a case-by-case basis. This comes in handy if you want to connect your iPad to the computer just to charge its battery and not to sync information. To prevent automatically syncing on a case-by-case basis, immediately after connecting your iPad, press the **Option** and **⌘** keys on your Mac keyboard at the same time until iPad appears in the Devices list. Press **Ctrl** and **Shift** for a PC. This aborts the automatic sync.

Sync Your Contacts List

An efficient way to manage your contacts on your iPad is to manually sync groups of contacts from your computer. A manual sync enables you to choose what contact information you want to place on your iPad. This way, if you want to sync only your contacts of friends and family to your iPad, you can do so without syncing work contacts in the process.

① Connect your iPad to your computer.

iTunes automatically launches, and iPad appears in the Devices list.

② Click **iPad** in the Devices list.

The Summary screen appears.

③ Click the **Info** tab.

The Info pane opens.

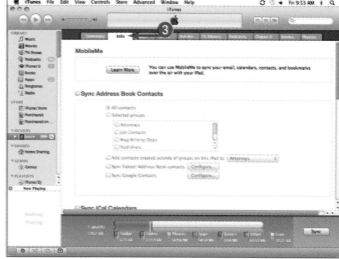

④ Click the **Sync Address Book Contacts** check box (☐ changes to ☑).

Note: *In Windows, click the **Sync contacts with** check box (☐ changes to ☑) and then choose the program you want to use.*

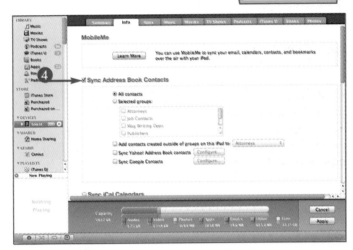

⑤ Click the **Selected groups** radio button (◌ changes to ◉).

⑥ Click only the groups you want to sync (☐ changes to ☑).

Note: *Only the contacts listed in the specific groups you choose are synced to your iPad.*

Note: *If you have a Yahoo or Google account and want to add your Yahoo address book to the sync, you can click **Sync Yahoo** and then follow the directions.*

⑦ Click **Apply**.

The groups that you have chosen are synced to your iPad.

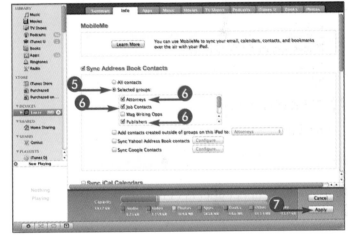

What can I do if I have problems syncing?

If you have problems syncing your Contacts, try going to the other tabs and deactivating sync for other content, such as music and movies. Configuring iTunes to sync only one type of data may solve the sync issue. Of course, if the problem lies with some other data you are trying to sync, you will need to address it when you try to sync that content to your iPad.

What is a sync conflict?

Sync conflicts can arise when you make two different edits on the same information: once on your computer; the other on your iPad. For example, you may have changed the contact information in Address Book on your Mac and then made a different edit for the same contact in Contacts on your iPad. In this scenario, iTunes does not know which is the correct information. When this occurs, a Conflict Resolver dialog box opens. Follow the directions in this dialog box to solve the sync conflict.

Sync Your Calendar

You can sync the calendar information located in the iCal application on your Mac or Outlook Calendar on your Windows PC to your Calendar app on your iPad. This way, you can stay up to date with your most current appointment schedule while on the go with your iPad.

Sync Your Calendar

① Connect your iPad to your computer.

iTunes launches automatically on your computer. iPad appears in the Devices list.

② Click **iPad** in the Devices list.

The Summary screen appears.

③ Click the **Info** tab.

The Info pane opens.

④ Click the **Sync iCal Calendars** check box (☐ changes to ☑).

Note: In Windows, click Sync calendars with and then choose the program you want to use.

⑤ Click the **All calendars** radio button (○ changes to ◉) to sync all calendars.

Note: You can select Do not sync events older than 30 days to control how far back the calendar sync goes. You can also type another value in the Days field.

⑥ Click **Apply**.

The selected calendars are synced to your iPad.

TIP

I have multiple calendars. How do I select just one of them?

If you have multiple calendars, you can sync only the calendars you want by clicking the **Selected calendars** radio button (○ changes to ◉) in the Calendars field. After you make this selection, the field listing your other calendars is no longer grayed out. Click the check boxes (☐ changes to ☑) next to the calendars in the list that you want to sync.

☑ Sync iCal Calendars

○ All calendars
◉ Selected calendars:

☐ Home
☑ Work

Sync Your Email Account

iTunes makes it easy for you to sync email accounts, including your MobileMe account, Outlook, and Windows Mail, to your iPad. Syncing your Mac or PC email accounts with your iPad is a great way to stay up to date with email messages when you are on the move.

① Connect your iPad to your computer.

iTunes launches automatically on your computer. iPad appears in the Devices list.

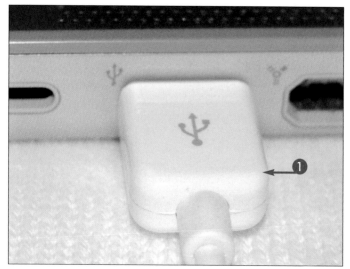

② Click **iPad** in the Devices list.

③ Click the **Info** tab.

The Info pane appears.

④ Click the **Sync Mail Accounts** check box (□ changes to ☑).

Note: In Windows, click the **Sync selected mail accounts from** check box (□ changes to ☑), choose your email program from the drop-down list, and then click the appropriate check box (□ changes to ☑) for each account.

⑤ Select the mail accounts you want to sync to your iPad.

⑥ Click **Apply**.

Note: Click **Allow** if you receive a message asking if AppleMobileSync can be allowed access to your keychain.

iTunes syncs the email accounts you have specified to your iPad.

If I have an email account already set up on my Mac or PC and not on my iPad, can I sync to configure my iPad with the new account?

Yes. An easy way to configure your iPad with an existing email account on your Mac or PC is to instruct iTunes to share the information with your iPad through syncing. During the sync, iTunes shares all the account information with your iPad and establishes the new account.

Sync Your Bookmarks

An easy way to get your bookmarks from your favorite websites over to your iPad is to sync them by using iTunes. When you sync your bookmarks, you are sharing the bookmarks that you have created within Safari or Internet Explorer on your Mac or PC so you can easily access those websites from your iPad.

Sync Your Bookmarks

① Connect your iPad to your computer.

iTunes launches automatically on your computer. iPad appears in the Devices list.

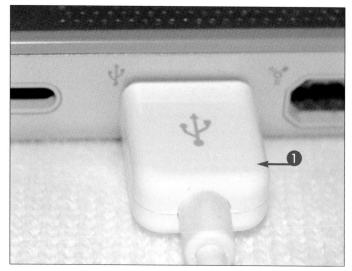

② Click **iPad** in the Devices list.

③ Click the **Info** tab.

The Info pane appears.

④ Scroll down to the Web Browser section and then click the **Sync Safari bookmarks** check box (☐ changes to ☑).

*Note: In Windows, click the **Sync bookmarks with** check box (☐ changes to ☑) and then select the web browser from the list.*

⑤ Click **Apply**.

Your bookmarks begin to sync from your computer to your iPad.

Any tips on syncing bookmarks?
Yes. Over time, you can accumulate many bookmarks on your computer. Some of these bookmarks may be to websites no longer relevant to you and that you no longer visit. Before you sync your bookmarks to your iPad, go through your bookmarks on your computer and then delete the ones no longer relevant. This way, you share only the important sites.

Sync Music and Music Videos

Your iPad is great for listening to music and watching music videos you may have downloaded from iTunes. If your iPad has the storage capacity to hold all the music and music videos you have downloaded to your computer, you can sync your entire library to your iPad. If you have a vast music library that exceeds the capacity of your iPad, you can configure iTunes to sync only the playlists, artists, genres, and videos that you want to share with your iPad.

Sync Music and Music Videos

Note: *You should already have your iPad connected to your computer before following these steps.*

① Click **iPad** in the Devices list.

② Click the **Music** tab.

The Music tab options appear.

③ Click the **Sync Music** check box
(☐ changes to ☑).

Note: *iTunes may ask you to confirm that you want to sync music.*

④ Click the **Selected playlist, artists, and genres** radio button (○ changes to ⦿).

⑤ Select the playlists, artists, or genres you want to sync by clicking the check box next to them (☐ changes to ☑).

⑥ Click the **Include music videos** check box (☐ changes to ☑) to include them into the sync.

⑦ Click **Apply**.

The playlists, artists, and genres you have selected are synced to your iPad.

TIP

Can I transfer individual songs that I want to my iPad?
Yes. You can manage your music manually by connecting your iPad to your computer and then clicking **Music** in the Source list. You can drag the individual songs that you want from your music library and then drop them on top of iPad in the Devices list to sync just those songs.

Sync
Podcasts

You can sync your favorite podcasts to your iPad so you can take them with you. Podcasts can range from just a few megabytes in size to tens of megabytes that can begin to eat into your iPad's storage space. When you pick and choose only the podcasts that you want to sync to your iPad, you are using your storage capacity wisely.

Sync Podcasts

Note: You should already have your iPad connected to your computer before following these steps.

① Click **iPad** in the Devices list.

② Click the **Podcasts** tab.

The Podcasts options appear.

③ Click the **Sync Podcasts** check box (☐ changes to ☑).

④ Click the **Automatically include** menu to choose an option.

⑤ Click the **selected podcasts** menu to choose an option.

You can now choose individual podcasts contained within the available podcast series.

⑥ Click a podcast in the Podcasts field.

The podcast is highlighted, and the individual episodes appear to the right.

⑦ Select each individual episode that you want to sync to your iPad.

Note: *If you want all the episodes that appear to the right of the podcast, you can just click the check box next to the podcast (☐ changes to ☑).*

Note: *Repeat steps 6 and 7 to choose new podcasts and individual episodes.*

⑧ Click **Apply**.

iTunes syncs the iPad with the specified podcast episodes.

TIP

Can I designate a podcast as unplayed?

Yes. A podcast is designated as unplayed if you have not played at least part of it in iTunes or on your iPad. If you play a podcast episode on your iPad, that information is relayed to iTunes the next time that you sync. You can mark an episode as unplayed by clicking **Podcasts** in the iTunes library, right-clicking on a particular podcast, and then choosing **Mark as Unplayed** from the menu.

> Play
>
> Mark as Played
> Mark as Unplayed
>
> Update Podcast
> Show all available episodes
> Subscribe Podcast
> Allow Auto Delete

Sync Audiobooks

You can sync audiobooks that you have downloaded to your computer to your iPad. Although Audiobooks does not have a tab like Music, Podcasts, and TV Shows, you can access audiobooks from under the Music tab. Syncing audiobooks is a great way to take your books with you while you travel.

Sync Audiobooks

Note: You should already have your iPad connected to your computer before following these steps.

1 Click **iPad** in the Devices list.

2 Click the **Books** tab.

The Books options appear.

3 Click the **Sync AudioBooks** check box (☐ changes to ☑).

④ Click the All audiobooks radio button (⊙ changes to ⊙).

⑤ Click **Apply**.

The audiobooks are synced to your iPad.

TIPS

If I have more than one audiobook, can I choose which ones I want to sync?

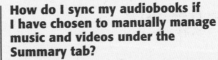

Yes. The names of the authors also appear in the Artists field. You can click the check box (□ changes to ☑) next to the name of the author in the Artists field to choose only the audiobooks that you want to sync to your iPad. Because you will probably have more musical artists than authors in this list, you can quickly find your authors by typing their names into the Search field located above the Artists field.

How do I sync my audiobooks if I have chosen to manually manage music and videos under the Summary tab?

If you have chosen the manual option under the Summary tab, the Playlists, Artists, and Genres options are not available under the Music tab. You will have to click the **Books** category in the iTunes library and then drag and drop the audiobooks that you want onto your iPad in the Devices list.

Sync TV Show Episodes

You can sync TV shows that you have downloaded to your computer to your iPad. If you have downloaded many TV episodes, such as if you have subscribed to an entire season of a program, you could quickly fill up your iPad's storage capacity. You can choose to sync only a select few episodes to your iPad to conserve storage capacity.

Note: *You should already have your iPad connected to your computer before following these steps.*

1 Click **iPad** in the Devices list.

2 Click the **TV Shows** tab.

The TV Shows options appear.

3 Click the **Sync TV Shows** check box (☐ changes to ☑).

4 Click the **Automatically include** menu to choose an option.

Note: *This example uses the default setting.*

⑤ Click the **selected shows** menu to choose an option.

You can now choose individual TV shows contained within the available TV series.

⑥ Click a TV show in the Shows list.

The TV show is highlighted, and the individual episodes appear to the right.

⑦ Select each individual episode that you want to sync to your iPad.

Note: *If you want all the episodes that appear to the right of the TV show, you can just select the check box next to the show (☐ changes to ☑).*

Note: *Repeat steps **6** and **7** to choose new TV shows and individual episodes.*

⑧ Click **Apply**.

iTunes syncs the iPad with the specified TV show episodes.

Can I designate a TV episode as unplayed?
Yes. A TV episode is designated as unplayed if you have not played at least part of it in iTunes or on your iPad. If you play a TV episode on your iPad, that information is relayed to iTunes the next time that you sync. You can mark an episode as unplayed by clicking the **TV Shows** tab in the iTunes library, right-clicking on a particular episode, and then choosing **Mark as Unwatched** from the menu.

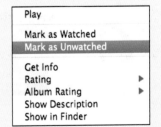

Sync Photos on Your Computer with Your iPad

The iPad camera connection kit accessory is a great way to transfer photos from your camera to your iPad. If you already have a collection of your favorite photos located on your computer, you can sync your favorite photos on your computer to your iPad. Syncing photos on your computer with your iPad is a great way to show off your photos when you travel.

Sync Photos on Your Computer with Your iPad

Note: *You should already have your iPad connected to your computer before following these steps.*

1 Click **iPad** in the Devices list.

2 Click the **Photos** tab.

The Photo options appear.

3 Click the **Sync Photos from** check box (☐ changes to ☑).

④ Choose an option from the pop-up menu.

Note: *This example uses **iPhoto**. You can also specify a folder by selecting **Choose folder**. In Windows, you can choose **My Pictures** or **Pictures**.*

Note: *What you choose here dictates the remaining steps. Because this example uses iPhoto, the following steps are for iPhoto.*

⑤ Click the **Selected albums and events, and automatically include** radio button (○ changes to ⦿).

Note: *You can click the **Include videos** check box (□ changes to ☑) if you have recorded video in your photo album that you want to include.*

⑥ Click the check boxes (□ changes to ☑) for the events you want to sync to your iPad.

⑦ Click **Apply**.

The photo album you have selected syncs to your iPad.

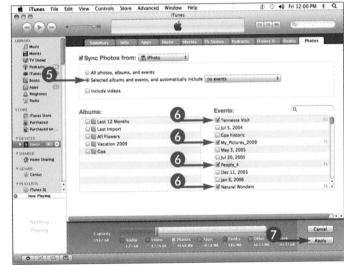

TIP

What file types are compatible with my iPad?
Your iPad is compatible with the usual TIFF and JPEG file formats along with PNG, BMP, and GIF files. If you have photos that are not compatible with your iPad, you will need to convert them to a compatible format before you can successfully sync them to your iPad.

Save Photos from Emails

Occasionally, friends and family members may send you an email with a photo attachment. Your iPad displays photo attachments in the following formats: JPEG, GIF, and TIFF. You can view that photo directly in the body of the email that you received, and you can also download the image and save it on your iPad.

Save Photos from Emails

① Tap **Mail** on the Home screen.

Your default email account opens.

② Open the email that contains the photo you want to download.

③ Tap the attachment.

The photo downloads and displays in the email message.

Note: If the image is in a format incompatible with your iPad, you can see the name of the file, but you cannot download it.

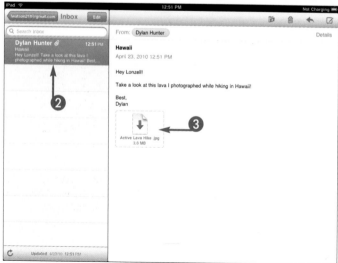

④ Tap the **Share** button (◀).

The options to **Reply**, **Forward**, or **Save Image** appear.

⑤ Tap **Save Image**.

The image is saved to a photo album and can be accessed with the Photos app.

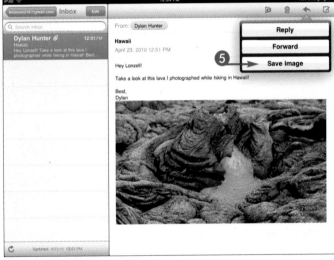

TIPS

Can I save video that I receive from an attachment?

Yes. But it needs to be an .mp4 file. You can save video attachments sent to you by email much in the same way that you save photos. Just tap and hold the video attachment until the menu opens, giving you the option to save the video. Tap **Save Video** to save the video to your iPad.

Can I save an image on a website?

Yes. You can save an image that you find on a website to your iPad. After you open the webpage that contains the image, tap and hold the image until you are given the option to save the image. Tap **Save Image** to save the website image to your iPad.

Import Photos from Your Camera

You have a number of options for importing your favorite photos to your iPad. You can sync photos on your computer to your iPad, you can collect them from email messages and websites, and you can also use the iPad camera connection kit to download photos directly from your camera. The iPad camera connection kit enables you to connect your camera to your iPad by USB cable or by simply inserting a memory card into an attached SD card reader to import images.

Import Photos from Your Camera

Connect with a USB Cable

1. Connect the USB to Dock adapter to the bottom of your iPad.

2. Attach one end of the USB cable into the adapter and the other end into the camera.

Note: *The camera should be turned on and placed into Still Image mode if needed.*

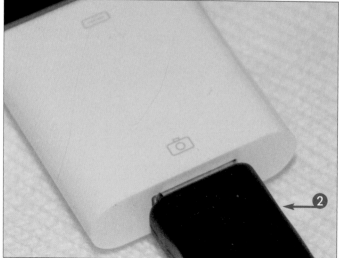

Connect an SD Card Connector

1. Connect the SD card reader to the 30-pin connector at the bottom of the iPad.

2. Insert the SD card from the camera into the slot.

Download Images

1. Click **Import All**.

   The images begin to transfer.

TIP

Can I use an Apple USB keyboard with the iPad by attaching it with the USB connector in the camera connection kit?

No. But you can purchase an Apple Wireless Keyboard that uses Bluetooth technology with your iPad. As long as you are within range — around 30 feet of your iPad — you can move around freely with this keyboard. You may also want to consider the Apple iPad keyboard dock, which enables you to charge your iPad while using a full-sized keyboard.

Getting the Most from iTunes and Photos

Your iPad is packed with entertainment possibilities. You can use iTunes to preview, purchase, and download music, movies, TV shows, podcasts, and audiobooks. The Photos app offers a variety of ways to import and showcase your photos, including photo albums, slideshows, and using your iPad itself as a picture frame. In this chapter, you learn the features of iTunes as well as how to set up an account, purchase and download content, and create playlists.

Discover What You Can Do
   with iTunes...138

Buy and Download in iTunes.........................140

Subscribe to Podcasts....................................142

Rate Content in the iTunes Store 144

Configure iPad Audio Settings 146

Browse and Play Content in
   the iPod App...148

Create a Standard Playlist in
   the iPod App...150

Play Videos, Movies, and TV Shows.............152

Customize Video Settings 154

View Photos on Your iPad..............................156

Send a Photo by Email 158

Create a Custom Slideshow 160

Purchasing Content

The iTunes Store has a wide variety of content to browse, including music, movies, TV shows, podcasts, audiobooks, games, and apps. Some content is free. Much of the content can be reviewed before you purchase, and you also have access to product descriptions and reviews from individuals who have previously purchased the content. Before you can make a purchase in the iTunes Store, you need to set up an iTunes account. Once you have set up an iTunes account, purchasing and downloading content is as simple as a few taps of your finger. You can scroll to the bottom of any page within iTunes and then tap **Sign In** to begin setting up an iTunes account.

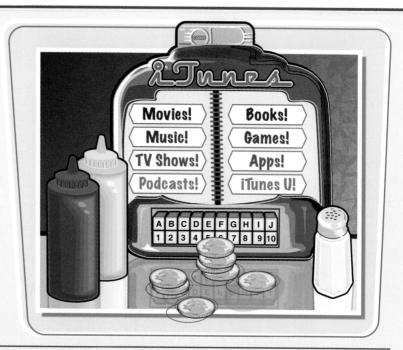

Organizing Content

Once you start downloading music, videos, and other content from iTunes, you can quickly amass a large library of content. iTunes is also a media management app that provides a number of ways to help you organize your content so that it is easy to find and use.

Using Playlists to Manage Your Library

Creating playlists in iTunes is not only a great way to create a compilation of your favorite songs for playback, but playlists also provide you with further organization. You can use three types of playlists on your iPad: Standard Playlists, Genius Playlists, and Genius Mixes. You can make playlists from the music, podcasts, or audiobooks in your iTunes library. Understanding how to create a playlist can help you get the most from the iPod app on your iPad.

Syncing Your Content

iTunes makes it easy for you to sync/share music, movies, TV shows, podcasts, audiobooks, email accounts, contacts, and calendars between multiple devices (iPhone, iPod, and iPad). You can also sync your MobileMe account or Outlook and Windows Mail to your iPad so you can check them while on the go and have easy access to current email messages.

Buy and Download in iTunes

After you have set up your iTunes account, purchasing and downloading music, movies, TV shows, and other content are very easy tasks. Once you understand how to purchase and download content from iTunes, you can begin to populate your iPad with a wide variety of entertaining and educational content. The process for downloading free content is almost identical.

Buy and Download in iTunes

① Tap **iTunes** on the Home screen.

iTunes opens.

② Navigate to the content that you want to purchase.

③ Tap the price next to the content that you want.

The Price button changes to the Buy button.

Note: *The Buy button is contextual, so if you are purchasing an album, it reads Buy Album. If you are buying a single, it reads Buy Single.*

④ Tap the **Buy** button.

If you are not signed in or do not have an iTunes account, a Sign In screen appears.

⑤ Tap **Use Existing Account** if you already have an iTunes account.

The iTunes Password dialog box opens.

Note: *If you do not have an iTunes account, tap **Create New Account** to create an iTunes account.*

⑥ Type your username.

⑦ Type your password.

⑧ Tap **OK**.

iTunes begins to download your purchase.

Note: *If the iTunes terms and conditions have changed, you may be prompted to read the new terms and conditions. If so, tap **OK**, read the terms and conditions, and then tap **Agree**. You will then have to attempt your purchase again.*

 TIP

Can I transfer and play purchased content from iTunes on my other computers?

Yes. You can play content that you have purchased on iTunes on up to five authorized computers, either Mac or Windows or both. Authorization is used to protect the copyright of purchased content on iTunes. In order to authorize a computer, you must open iTunes on that computer, choose **Store**, and then choose **Authorize Computer** from the main menu bar. You will be required to type the password to your iTunes Store account. Devices such as an iPad, iPod, or iPhone do not count as a computer. You can deauthorize a computer by choosing **Store** and then choose **Deauthorize Computer** from the main menu bar.

Subscribe to Podcasts

Podcasts are downloadable radio- and TV-style shows. iTunes has a wide variety of audio and video podcasts, ranging from old-time radio classics to sports, science, and your favorite television shows. You can use iTunes to download podcasts straight to your iPad. Most podcasts are free, and you do not need an iTunes account to play or download podcasts.

① Tap **iTunes** on the Home screen.

iTunes opens.

② Tap **Podcasts** on the iTunes menu bar at the bottom.

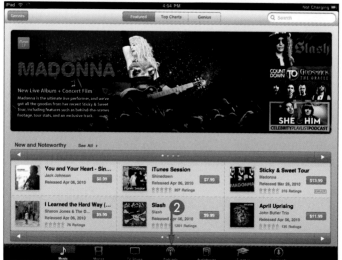

The Podcasts categories appear.

③ Navigate to a podcast that you want to download and then tap the podcast.

The podcast description appears, along with a list of the individual episodes.

Note: *If you tap on a banner for a genre of podcasts, you are taken to a screen that displays all the available podcasts.*

④ Tap the **Free** button for the episode that you want to download.

The Free button turns into the Get Episode button.

⑤ Tap **Get Episode**.

iTunes begins downloading the episode.

⑥ Repeat steps **3** and **4** to download more episodes.

Note: *You can now close iTunes and then open the iPod app on your iPad to begin listening to your podcasts.*

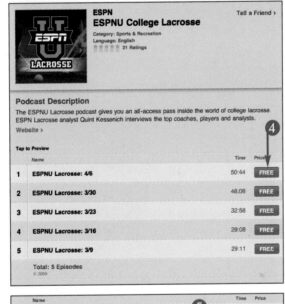

 TIPS

Can I subscribe to podcasts on my iPad?

No. But you can subscribe to a podcast within iTunes on your computer and then sync the new episodes to your iPad, iPhone, and iPod. Subscribing to your favorite podcast is a great way to have new episodes automatically download to your computer as they become available. You can also automatically update your podcast subscriptions from your computer.

What if I am unable to subscribe to a podcast?

If a podcast does not begin to download after you tap the Get Episode button, the website that hosts the podcast may be experiencing difficulties, so you might want to try again later. Another thing to consider is that some podcasts may use files incompatible with iTunes and iPad. It is rare, but if you suspect this, you should contact the producer of the podcast to receive more information.

Rate Content in the iTunes Store

iTunes uses a five-star rating system to rate all content. Just about all the content on iTunes features reviews that you can read to see how others like the product. You can easily write reviews of your own to make your feelings known about the content you have purchased. Rating content you have purchased on iTunes helps others to make educated decisions about their purchases on iTunes.

Rate Content in the iTunes Store

① Tap **iTunes** on the Home screen.

iTunes opens.

② Navigate to the content that you want to rate and then tap it.

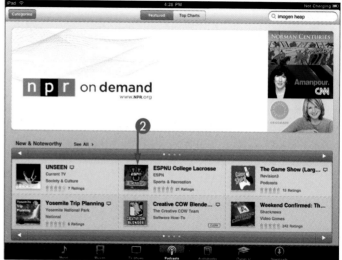

The content description page appears.

③ Scroll down toward the bottom of the content description page and then tap **Write a Review**.

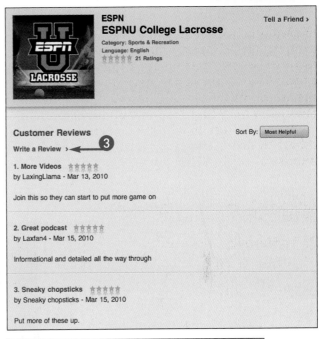

iTunes takes you to the Write a Review page.

Note: *If you are not logged in, iTunes prompts you to type your iTunes password. Log in to your account and then tap **OK**.*

④ Tap the number of stars you give the content.

⑤ Type the title of your review.

⑥ Type your nickname.

⑦ Type your review.

⑧ Tap **Submit**.

The review is uploaded to iTunes.

 TIP

Can I rate content that I have not purchased on iTunes?

Yes. But unless you have experience with the product you are reviewing, you probably should not do this. Many individuals use the ratings and feedback you supply to make purchasing choices on iTunes, so it is best to provide the most accurate and sincere review possible.

Configure iPad Audio Settings

The iPod app on your iPad is where you can listen to your music, podcasts, and audiobooks. Your iPad gives you the opportunity to adjust settings for audio playback in the iPad app. Using the iPod app preferences enables you to customize your audio experiences on the iPad.

① Tap **Settings** on the Home screen.

The Settings screen appears.

② Tap **iPod**.

The iPod settings appear.

③ Tap **Sound Check** to the **On** position to have iTunes play songs at the same level.

④ Tap **EQ**.

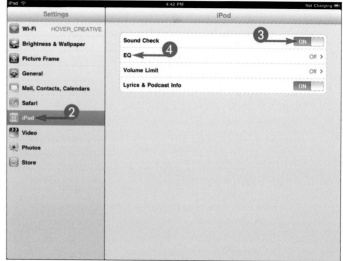

The EQ options appear.

Note: The EQ options are audio presets that you can choose to customize audio playback on your iPad.

5 Tap an EQ option to select it.

● A check mark appears next to the option you have chosen.

6 Tap **iPod**.

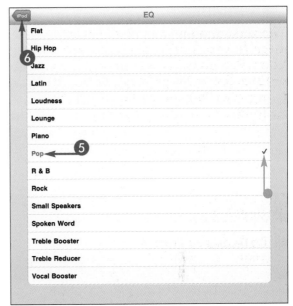

iPad returns to the iPod settings screen.

Note: You can leave Lyrics & Podcast Info to On to display lyrics and podcast information.

7 Tap **Volume Limit** to set a maximum volume at which audio can be played back on your iPad.

The Volume Limit slider appears.

8 Drag the slider to the desired level.

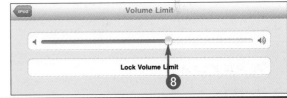

 TIP

Is there any way that I can keep the Volume Limit from being changed once I set it?

Yes. You can set the Volume Limit by dragging the slider and then create a passcode that would need to be typed in order to change it. It is important that you remember the passcode. Follow these steps:

1 Tap **Lock Volume Limit** in the Volume Limit options.

2 Type a four-digit passcode.

3 Type the four-digit passcode again.

The Volume Limit is locked.

4 Tap **Unlock Volume Limit** and then retype the passcode to unlock the volume limit.

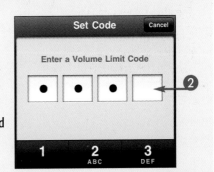

Browse and Play Content in the iPod App

The iPod app on your iPad was designed to make it easy for you to browse your music collection, podcasts, and audiobooks on your iPad. You can use the built-in speaker in your iPad to play back content or use a set of headphones. The ability to browse your iPod content library is the first step toward getting the most from the iPod app.

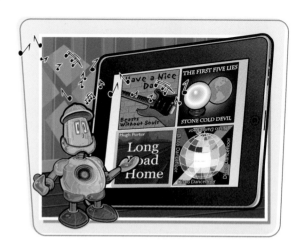

Browse and Play Content in the iPod App

① Tap **iPod** on the Home screen.

The iPod app opens.

② Tap the category for the content that you want to browse in the iPod library.

The contents for the category appear on the right-hand side of the screen.

Note: *This example uses the Music category.*

Note: *Use your finger to scroll up and down the results in the list.*

Note: *For the Music and Purchased categories, you can sort content by Songs, Artists, Albums, Genres, and Composers.*

③ Tap a song in the list to play it.

The Now Playing screen appears. The album cover fills the screen.

④ Tap the screen once to reveal the playback controls.

Note: *You can use the repeat and shuffle controls to repeat the song after it finishes or shuffle the songs in the library.*

Note: *The next song in the list plays automatically after the current song ends. Tap **Albums** on the menu bar at the bottom of the screen to play all the songs from a specific album.*

TIP

Can I play music in the background and access the playback controls while using another app?

Yes. As a song is playing, you can press the **Home** button (⬜) to return to the Home screen and open another app. You can quickly press ⬜ twice to reveal the playback controls.

Create a Standard Playlist in the iPod App

Playlists are a great way to create a compilation of your favorite songs for playback in iTunes. You can use three types of playlists on your iPad: Standard Playlists, Genius Playlists, and Genius Mixes. You can make playlists from the music, podcasts, or audiobooks in your iPod library. Understanding how to create a playlist can help you get the most from the iPod app on your iPad.

Standard Playlist
- The First Five Lies
- The Long Road Home
- I Thought I Knew You
- Who Am I?
- The Life You Wanted
- My First Kiss
- Hello, Baby, Hello!
- The Good Old Days
- My Summer Alone
- High School Hero
- New Beginnings

Create a Standard Playlist in the iPod App

① Tap **iPod** on the Home screen.

The iPod app opens.

② Tap the **Music** category in the iPod library.

The music on your iPad appears on the right.

③ Tap the Plus icon (＋) in the bottom-left corner of the screen.

The New Playlist dialog box opens, and iTunes prompts you to type a name for the new playlist.

4 Type the name for the new playlist.

5 Tap **Save**.

iPad takes you back to the Music library.

6 Tap the songs that you want to add to the playlist.

The songs gray out when you tap them and are then placed into the playlist.

7 Tap **Done** when you are finished.

The iPod app takes you to the new playlist you have created, and the playlist is in Edit mode.

Note: You can change the order of the songs by dragging the song tiles up and down, dropping them in their new position.

Note: Tap **Add Songs** to add more songs to the playlist.

Can I create a Genius list on my iPad?

Yes. You can create a Genius list and Genius Mixes on your iPad, but you first have to turn on Genius in iTunes on your computer. You then need to sync your iPad with iTunes. You can create a Genius Playlist in order to have iTunes automatically play a collection of songs of the same genre that go well together. After you have turned on Genius, you can create and save Genius playlists on your iPad. You need an iTunes Store account in order to create a Genius list.

Play Videos, Movies, and TV Shows

You can view movies, TV shows, music videos, and video podcasts by tapping **Videos** on the Home screen. Understanding how to navigate your video collection on your iPad enables you to locate and play your favorite videos from the comfort of your iPad.

① Tap **Videos** on the Home screen.

The Videos app opens.

② Tap **TV Shows** on the main menu bar at the top of the screen.

All the TV shows on your iPad are shown.

Note: You can also choose Movies, Podcasts, and Music Videos on this screen.

③ Tap the show that you want to play.

The individual episodes appear on the left of the screen, and the artwork for the TV show appears on the right.

Note: *If you tapped a movie under the Movies category, a movie description appears, supplying you with information about the downloaded file.*

④ Tap the episode that you want to play.

The episode begins playing.

Note: *You can also tap the **Play** button to begin playing all the episodes back to back.*

Note: *Consider watching videos in landscape orientation for the biggest picture.*

⑤ Tap the screen to reveal the playback controls.

TIP

Can I watch movies on my iPad on a television screen?

Yes. You can use the Apple Component AV cable, Composite AV Cable, Apple iPad Dock Connector to VGA Adapter, and other compatible connectors to connect your iPad to a TV or projector. The Apple cables and docks are sold separately. Make sure that you make the proper adjustments for the TV OUT settings by going to Settings under Video.

You can customize the video settings on your iPad to determine if videos start where you left off or if they should start at the beginning. You can also choose to turn on closed captioning and configure your iPod to play out to a TV set. The ability to customize the video options on your iPad gives you more viewing options.

Customize Video Settings

1 Tap **Settings** on the Home screen.

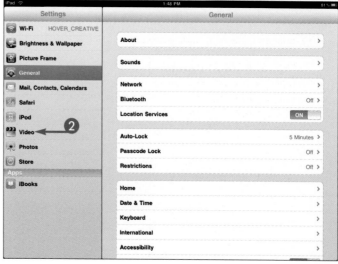

The Settings screen appears.

2 Tap **Video**.

The Video options appear.

③ Tap **Start Playing** to choose the starting point for videos after you have stopped them and want to replay them.

④ Tap **Closed Captioning** to the **On** position if you are hearing impaired.

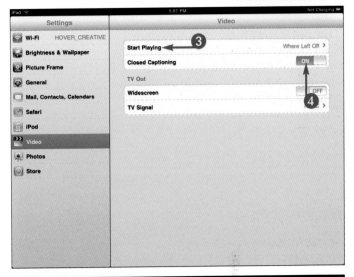

⑤ Tap **Widescreen** to the **On** position if you are playing widescreen video on your iPad out to a TV set.

⑥ Tap **TV Signal** to set whether the TV you are playing out to uses an NTSC or PAL signal.

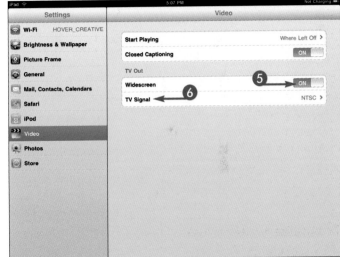

 TIP

What are NTSC and PAL?
NTSC (National Television System Committee) and PAL (Phase Alternating Line) are the two major standard analog television encoding systems used in broadcast television. NTSC is used in North America and Japan, and PAL is used nearly everywhere else in the world.

View Photos on Your iPad

The Photos app enables you to view photos you have synced from your computer or downloaded from your camera or a memory card. Photos can be managed as albums, events, faces, and places and are showcased in a high-quality display. Your iPad supports the JPEG, GIF, and PNG photo formats. Knowing the options of how to view your photos enables you to get the most from your photography on your iPad.

View Photos on Your iPad

① Tap **Photos** on the Home screen.

The Photos app opens.

② Tap the category of pictures you want to view.

③ Tap a collection to open it.

The collection of photos opens, revealing its contents.

Note: *You can also pinch your fingers shut on-screen to collapse the collection of photos again.*

④ Tap the photo that you want to view.

The photo opens.

Note: *Notice the controls that appear at the top and bottom of the page. You can use the controls at the bottom of the screen to tap and open a new photo. The controls disappear after a few seconds or you can tap the screen once to make the controls disappear.*

⑤ Tap a thumbnail at the bottom of the page to progress to the next photo.

Note: *You can also turn the page with your finger to progress to the next picture.*

Note: *You can rotate the iPad to the proper orientation to view the photo.*

Note: *You can double-tap the photo to make it larger. Double-tap it again to have it return to its original size.*

Note: *You can perform a pinching motion with two fingers on-screen to enlarge the photograph and then pan the photo with one finger.*

Can I upload photos to my MobileMe Gallery?

Yes. You can even add photos to someone else's MobileMe account. First, you need to set up your MobileMe account on your iPad. Second, you need to publish a MobileMe Gallery and configure it to allow photos from iPad. If you do not have a MobileMe account, you can set up one at www.me.com.

Send a Photo by Email

The Photos app provides a great way to view and organize your photos. The Photos app also makes it very easy to share your photographs with others by emailing them to friends and family. In just a few taps, you can create a new email and place a photo in the body of the letter.

Complete these steps with the Photos app already open.

Send a Photo by Email

1 Tap the photo collection that contains the picture you want to mail.

The photo collection opens.

2 Tap the photo that you want to mail.

The photo opens.

③ Tap the **Share** button ().

A menu appears.

Note: You may need to first tap the screen to make appear.

④ Tap **Email Photo**.

Note: You can also use this menu to add a photo to a contact or choose a photo as the wallpaper for your iPad.

A new email message is created, with the photo in the body of the letter.

⑤ Type the email address of the recipient.

⑥ Type a subject.

Note: You can type a message in the body of the letter if desired. An easy way to type the body of the letter is to tap the picture once. A blue cursor appears to the right of the picture. Press the Return key on the keyboard. The cursor appears underneath the picture, and you can begin typing.

⑦ Tap **Send**.

The message is sent to the recipient.

TIP

Does my iPad have screen saver capabilities?

Yes. The feature is called Picture Frame. When your iPad is locked, an icon of a sunflower appears to the right of Slide to Unlock. When you tap that icon, iPad uses photos in your photo library as a slideshow while your iPad charges in the dock. You can adjust the settings of Picture Frame by tapping **Settings** on the Home screen. Under Settings, you can choose the type of transition you want between slides, the duration of the slides, a specific collection of photos for the slideshow, and more.

Create a Custom Slideshow

You can create a custom slideshow by choosing your own music and transitions between photographs in the Photos app. Creating a customized slideshow is a quick way to preview a newly imported group of pictures on your iPad and then add your own personal touch.

Create a Custom Slideshow

1 Tap **Photos** on the Home screen.

The Photos app opens.

2 Tap the photo collection that you want to view as a slideshow.

The photo collection opens.

③ Tap **Slideshow**.

The Slideshow options appear.

④ Tap **Music**.

The music contained in your Music library appears.

⑤ Locate the music that you want to use and tap the track.

The Music library closes.

⑥ Tap **Start Slideshow**.

The slideshow begins to play full screen.

Note: *Tap the screen once to stop the slideshow.*

Can I set the duration for my slideshow?
Yes. You can change the duration for each slide, determine whether the slideshow repeats after it has finished playing, and set photos to shuffle. Follow these steps:

① Tap **Settings** on the Home screen.

② Tap **Photos**.

③ Customize the individual slideshow settings.

Photos	
Slideshow	
Play Each Slide For	3 Seconds >
Repeat ← ③	OFF
Shuffle	OFF

Getting the Most from YouTube and iBooks

Your iPad is an entertainment center packed with many options for you to experience the web and download materials for your own personal enjoyment. Your iPad is a highly capable e-reader with the ability to browse, purchase, and download books with the iBooks app. Your YouTube experience has been optimized for your viewing pleasure on the iPad. In this chapter, you learn how to utilize the features of YouTube and iBooks so you can get the most from both of these apps.

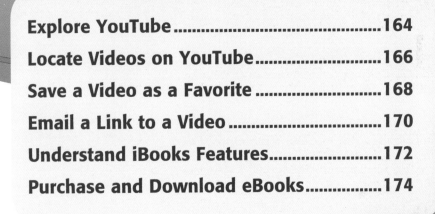

Explore YouTube 164

Locate Videos on YouTube 166

Save a Video as a Favorite 168

Email a Link to a Video 170

Understand iBooks Features 172

Purchase and Download eBooks 174

YouTube is a video-sharing website that gives you the ability to browse and view videos posted by users from around the world. Before you can upload a video from your computer, you need to create a YouTube account. The iPad offers a great way to experience videos on YouTube. Understanding some of the features of YouTube can help you optimize your YouTube experience on the iPad.

View Videos

There are literally millions of free videos on YouTube for you to enjoy. They span a wide range of categories, from entertainment to politics to educational. Users can upload and view standard-definition videos as well as high-definition videos. If you have young children that may use your iPad, you should consider configuring parental controls to protect them from any unsavory videos.

Share Videos

YouTube makes it easy for you to showcase your videos to millions of viewers around the world by creating your own video channel. YouTube also makes it easy for you to share videos found on YouTube by embedding them in your own personal blog. You also have the ability to email videos to family and friends by simply tapping the Mail button and then typing the address of the recipient.

Subscribe to Channels

If you are a fan of the videos produced by a particular YouTube user, you can simply subscribe to that individual's channel. That way, whenever that user posts a new video, you will receive a notification. Subscribing to channels is a quick and easy way to access the work of your favorite YouTube personalities.

Express Your Opinion

YouTube makes it easy for you to voice your opinion by enabling you to leave comments for videos and rate videos as well as rate comments left by fellow YouTube viewers. Some of the popular videos on YouTube can generate literally thousands of comments, which ultimately lead to conversations. You can use the YouTube five-star rating system to assess the popularity of a particular video before you watch.

Join Groups

YouTube also makes it easy for you to connect with other like-minded individuals through the creation and joining of groups. Joining groups is a great way for you to contribute your thoughts on interesting videos and conversations that happen every day on YouTube. Once you join a group, it is easy to create new topics of discussion.

Locate Videos on YouTube

To say there is a lot of content on YouTube is an understatement. The YouTube app on the iPad helps you locate videos of interest in a variety of ways by organizing content. The YouTube app enables you to search by Featured, Most Viewed, Search, and Favorites. You can tap the More button to reveal other browsing options.

● **Featured**
Tap this button to access a list of videos handpicked by YouTube editors. Each video is listed with its name, star rating, popularity, and duration.

● **Top Rated**
Tap this button to list the videos with the highest ratings on YouTube. Under this button, there are more ways to browse video by filtering the top rated videos for Today, This Week, and All.

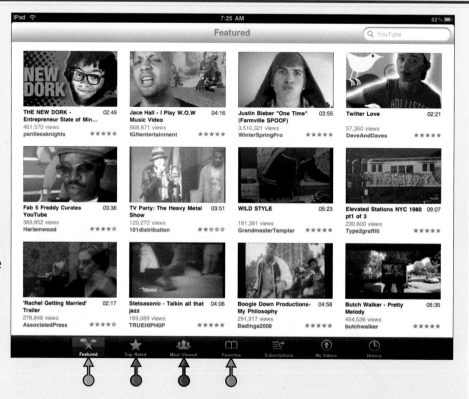

● **Most Viewed**
Tap this button to see videos with the most views by users and visitors to YouTube. You can narrow this search by choosing Today, This Week, and All. Under this button, there are more ways to browse video by filtering the most viewed videos of Today, This Week, and All.

● **Favorites**
This option requires some previous work on your part. Tap this button to display the videos you have previously bookmarked and marked as favorites. You will also find the Playlist button under the Favorites option. Tap Playlist to view the playlists you have previously created on YouTube.

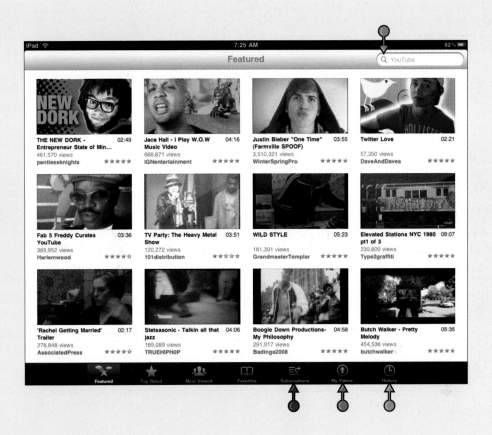

- **Subscriptions**
  You can tap this option to view a list of the channels to which you are subscribed.

- **My Videos**
  Tap this button to view a list of the videos you have previously uploaded to YouTube.

- **History**
  You can tap this option to view a list of videos you have previously watched on YouTube.

- **Search**
  Tap this button to access a search box. You can type a search phrase into the field, and YouTube displays the videos that match your search.

Save a Video as a Favorite

When you find a video that you really like, the YouTube app makes it easy for you to mark it as a favorite. Marking a video as a favorite enables you to easily find that video for viewing again without relying on your viewing history or the Search feature.

Save a Video as a Favorite

① Tap **YouTube** on the Home screen.

The YouTube app opens.

② Locate the video that you want to save as a favorite and then tap the video to begin playback.

The video begins to play.

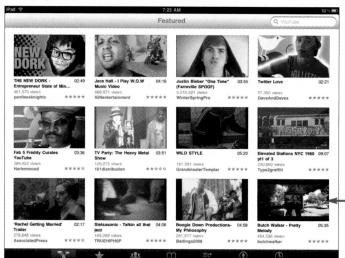

3 Tap the **Bookmarks** icon (📖).

The 📖 turns gray, and iPad creates a bookmark for the video.

Note: If you do not see the controls, you may have to tap the screen to reveal them.

4 Tap **Done**.

The video stops, and you are taken to the More Info screen.

Note: You can also just wait until the video ends before you proceed.

The video now appears in the Favorites list.

TIP

Can I delete videos that I have previously marked as favorite?
Yes. While accessing your favorites page, you can do the following:

1 Tap the **Edit** button.

An X is placed next to each video in the list.

The Save As dialog box opens.

2 Tap **Delete**.

3 Tap **OK**.

The video is removed from the list.

4 Tap **Done**.

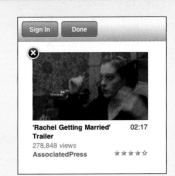

Email a Link to a Video

The YouTube app makes it very easy to share some of your favorite videos with friends and family. By understanding how to email a link to a video through the iPad, you can quickly share a great video that you found.

Email a Link to a Video

① Tap **YouTube** on the Home screen.

The YouTube app opens.

② Turn your iPad into portrait orientation and then tap **Favorites**.

The videos you have marked as favorites appear.

③ Tap the video you want to email.

The Share option appears.

Note: In order to see the share option, you have to be in the video detail page.

④ Tap **Share**.

A new email message opens, with the link to the video in the body.

⑤ Type the recipient's email address.

Note: If the recipient is someone you have emailed from your iPad before, you can just choose him or her from the list.

Note: You can also modify the subject and the body.

⑥ Tap **Send**.

The message is sent to the recipient, and iPad sends you back to your video.

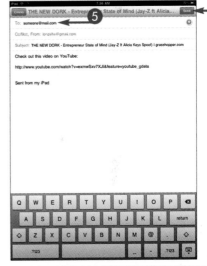

Can I mail a video to someone in my contact list?

Yes. But you need an email address included with the contact. After you tap the Mail button, follow these steps:

① Tap the **Plus** button (⊕).

Your Contacts list appears.

② Tap the recipient.

The recipient's name is placed into the To field within the email.

Note: You can also modify the subject and the body.

③ Tap **Send**.

The video is sent to the recipient.

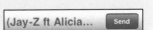

Understand iBooks Features

iBooks is a stylish e-reader that enables you to browse, purchase, download, and read eBooks very much in the same way as the Classics app. You can download iBooks for free in the App Store. Understanding what you can do with iBooks enables you to take full advantage of the iBooks software on the iPad.

Browse Titles

You can browse the sleek iBooks storefront for classics and bestsellers with a flick of your finger. iBooks has partnered with publishers such as Penguin, HarperCollins, Macmillan, and Simon & Schuster, giving you access to a wide array of bestsellers to choose from.

Purchase and Download Books

iBooks enables you to download free and paid eBooks much in the same way as iTunes allows you to download and purchase music. As you download books, their covers appear on your personal bookshelf. All you need to do to browse your own bookshelf is flick your finger up or down to scroll through your library. In order to purchase books, you need to set up an iBooks account.

Read Books

iPad is a very stylish and capable e-reader. You can simply tap a book on your shelf to begin reading. The page-turning animation gives you the effect of turning the actual book's pages with your hand. Each time you stop reading, iPad places a bookmark before the book is closed so you can later easily pick up where you stopped. The high-resolution, LED-backlit screen offers easy viewing in sharp clarity.

Edit Settings

The iPad also enables you to customize your reading experience by enabling you to edit some of the settings. You can edit what style of text you view as well as the font size to optimize your reading experience. The iPad attempts to maintain many of the characteristics of traditional book reading while giving you more options as an e-reading device.

Purchase and Download eBooks

Purchasing books in iBooks is very similar to purchasing content in the iTunes Store. By understanding how to purchase and download books in the iBooks app, you can begin filling your bookshelf with your favorite book titles. To purchase books in iBooks, you need to set up an iBooks account.

Purchase and Download eBooks

① Tap **iBooks** on the Home screen.

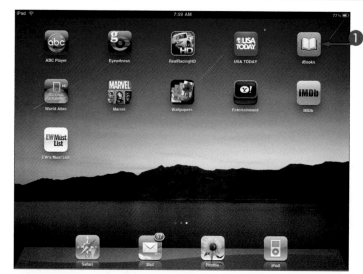

The iBooks app opens.

② Tap **Store**.

The iBooks Store opens.

③ Locate the book you want to purchase and download and then tap the Price.

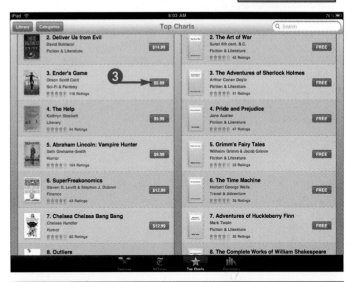

The icon changes to Buy Book.

Note: Tap Free for free books to download.

Note: The icon changes to Install after you tap it.

④ Tap the **Buy Book** icon.

iBooks asks you to type your iBooks account password.

⑤ Type your iBooks account password.

⑥ Tap **OK**.

iBooks begins to download the eBook. The book cover appears on your bookshelf.

TIP

Will I be charged twice if I attempt to download a book I have previously purchased?

Usually not. If you attempt to download a book that you have previously purchased, iBooks generally alerts you to this fact and asks if you would like to proceed with the download. If you are billed twice for the download, you can report a problem in the iBooks Store.

CHAPTER 9

Managing Contacts and Appointments

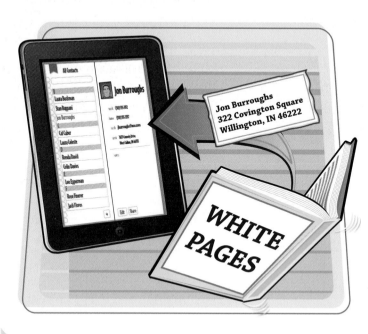

Your iPad is not just an entertainment center; it is also a highly capable tool to help you organize your life. The iPad is equipped with the Contacts and Calendar apps that help you improve your efficiency when it comes to managing personal contacts and important appointments. In this chapter, you learn how to use the Contacts and Calendar apps to help you stay organized.

Create a New Contact 178

Edit an Existing Contact 180

Assign an Email Address to a Contact 182

Assign a Web Address to a Contact............184

Assign a Physical Address to a Contact.....186

Create a Custom Label for a Contact..........188

Add Extra Fields for a Contact.....................190

Add Notes to a Contact 192

Add Photos to Contacts 194

Add Appointments to Your Calendar 196

Edit an Existing Appointment.......................198

Set Up a Repeating Event 200

Convert an Event to an All-Day Event 202

Add an Alert to an Event 204

Create a New Contact

The Contacts app can help you manage the important information you receive from friends, colleagues, and prospective business associates. Think of the Contacts app as your virtual Rolodex, filled with contact information such as names, physical addresses, emails, notes, and so on. Understanding how to create a new contact helps you to manage your personal contacts.

① Tap **Contacts** on the Home screen.

The Contacts app opens.

② Tap the **Plus** button (+).

A new contact screen appears.

A blinking cursor appears in the box labeled First.

③ Tap each field and then type the information you have for the contact.

Note: *If you want to note what type of phone line it is, tap the field labeled* **mobile** *and then choose from the list that appears.*

④ Tap **Done**.

Your iPad saves the information you have typed and takes you to the All Contacts screen.

Is it easy to delete a contact?

Yes. Follow these steps to delete a contact:

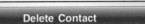

① Tap **Contacts** on the Home screen.

② Tap the contact you want to delete.

③ Tap **Edit** in the bottom-left corner of the page.

④ Scroll to the bottom of the contact sheet and then tap **Delete Contact**.

⑤ Tap **Delete Contact** again.

Edit an Existing Contact

The Contacts app makes it very easy to edit existing contacts. Understanding how to edit contacts enables you to quickly update information such as a contact's phone number or email address.

① Tap **Contacts** on the Home screen.

The Contacts app opens.

② Tap the contact you want to edit.

iPad displays the contact.

③ Tap **Edit**.

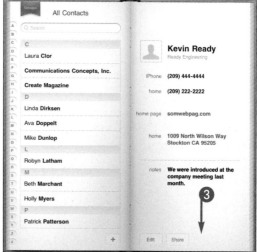

iPad displays the contact's data in the Info Screen. A red button (⊖) appears next to the data you can edit.

④ Tap the data field(s) that you want to edit and then make your edits.

The on-screen keyboard appears as you tap the field you want to edit.

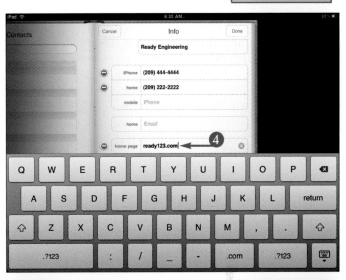

⑤ Tap **Done**.

Your iPad returns you to the All Contacts screen.

I have a lot of contacts. How do I quickly find the contact I need to edit?

You can use the Search field at the top of the All Contacts screen. As you begin to type the contact you are searching for, the results narrow until they match your search. In order to display all the contacts again, tap the ⊗ located in the Search field to clear the search.

All Contacts
Q Tim| ⊗
Tim Smith

Assign an Email Address to a Contact

It may not be possible to acquire all the contact information from an individual in one meeting; so, naturally, you will have to add it later. It is very common for an individual to have a work and home number and also an email address for work and one for personal use. The Contacts app makes it very easy for you to assign an email address to a contact.

① Tap **Contacts** on the Home screen.

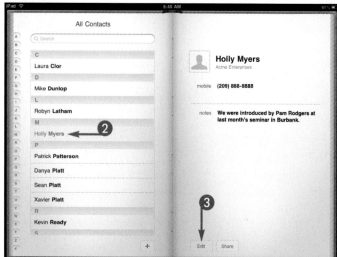

The Contacts app opens.

② Tap the contact to whom you want to assign an email address.

The contact's Info screen appears.

③ Tap **Edit**.

The Info screen appears.

④ Tap the **Email** field and then type the email address.

A blinking cursor appears in the Email field when you tap it, and the on-screen keyboard appears.

Note: *You can tap in the label field to change an email address's label.*

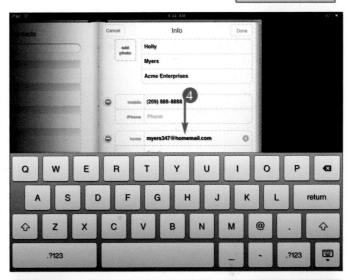

⑤ Tap **Done**.

The email address is saved as part of the contact information.

TIP

How do I save multiple email addresses?
As soon as you begin typing your first email address for a contact, a new Email field appears beneath it. The second field appears with a different label, so if your original email address has a Home label, iPad automatically labels the second email as Work and so on.

home	myers347@homemail.com
work	myers@myacme.com

Assign a Web Address to a Contact

It is now very common for individuals to have their own website and not just a telephone number, email address, or street address. The Contacts app makes it very easy for you to visit an individual's website just by tapping the URL on the Info screen.

Assign a Web Address to a Contact

① Tap **Contacts** on the Home screen.

The Contacts app opens.

② Tap the contact to whom you want to assign a web address.

The contact's Info screen appears.

③ Tap **Edit**.

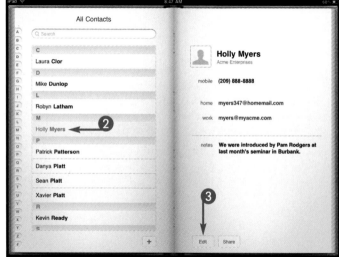

184

The Info screen appears.

4 Tap the **URL** field and then type the web address.

A blinking cursor appears in the URL field when you tap it, and the on-screen keyboard displays.

Note: *You can tap in the label field to change the label for the web address. By default, the label field reads home page.*

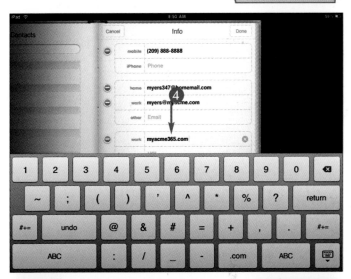

5 Tap **Done**.

The URL is saved as part of the contact information.

TIP

How do I assign multiple web addresses?

As soon as you begin typing your web address into the URL field, a new URL field appears beneath it. The second field appears with a different label.

work	**myacme365.com**	
home page	**homewebsite.com**	⊗

Assign a Physical Address to a Contact

Assigning a street address to a contact enables you to save an individual's address and access it quickly whenever you need it. It is very simple to add street addresses into the Contacts app so you can take advantage of these benefits.

① Tap **Contacts** on the Home screen.

The Contacts app opens.

② Tap the contact to whom you want to assign a physical address.

The contact's Info screen appears.

③ Tap **Edit**.

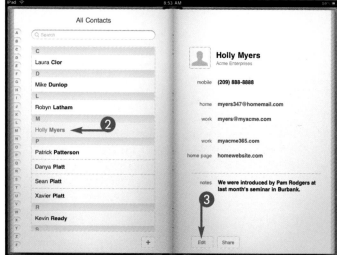

The Info screen appears.

④ Scroll down to tap the **add new address** field and then type an address.

A blinking cursor appears in the add new address field when you tap it, and the on-screen keyboard appears.

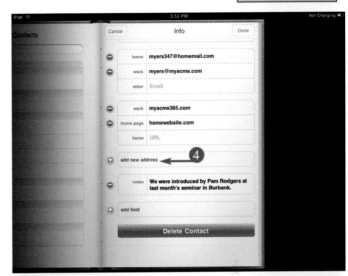

⑤ Tap **Done**.

The address is saved as part of the contact information.

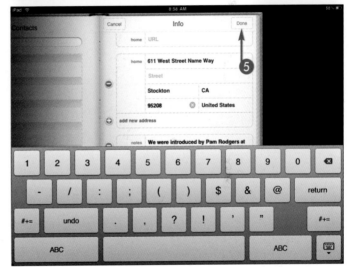

Can I see a map of the physical address I have assigned?

Yes. Another benefit to assigning an address to a contact is the fact that you can later use the Maps app to get a detailed map of the area just by tapping the address. You can tap the address for your contact to use the Maps app to quickly get directions to that location.

home	**611 West Street Name Way**
	Stockton CA 95208

Create a Custom Label for a Contact

Whenever you assign information to your contacts, your iPad requires that you identify certain information, such as a telephone number or physical address, with labels, such as home, work, mobile, and so on. Occasionally, one of these labels may prove too generic for your purposes. In this case, you can create your own labels to categorize your contact information.

Create a Custom Label for a Contact

1 Tap **Contacts** on the Home screen.

The Contacts app opens.

2 Tap the contact for whom you want to create a custom label.

The contact's Info screen appears.

3 Tap **Edit**.

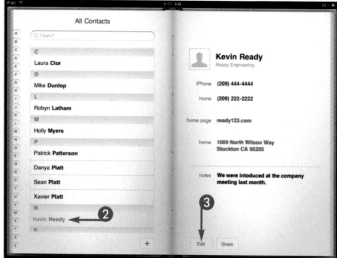

④ Tap the label for the contact data for which you will create the custom label.

Note: *For this example, I have chosen to change the label for an existing web address.*

The Label screen appears.

⑤ Tap **Add Custom Label**.

The Custom Label screen and the on-screen keyboard appear.

⑥ Type a new label.

⑦ Tap **Save**.

The custom label appears next to the data on the Info screen.

⑧ Repeat steps **4** to **7** to create custom labels for other data fields if needed.

Why can I not save my custom label for new data?

Before your iPad can save your custom label, you must edit or add the data and then save your work. Once you have typed your contact's data into the field, the custom label is saved along with the data in the All Contacts screen.

Info	Done

Do I have to re-create my custom label to use the same one again?

No. Once you create a custom label, you can access it again from the Label screen to use it for other contact data, such as phone numbers, email addresses, web addresses, and physical addresses.

Add Extra Fields for a Contact

When you add a new contact, by default, your iPad supplies you with only the basic data fields. Fortunately, your iPad has a collection of additional descriptive fields that you can access and apply to a contact's information. You can add extra fields, such as prefix for a Dr. or a suffix for Jr., Sr., III, and more.

Add Extra Fields for a Contact

① Tap **Contacts** on the Home screen.

The Contacts app opens.

② Tap the contact for which you want to add a new field.

The contact's Info screen appears.

③ Tap **Edit**.

The Info screen appears.

④ Scroll down and then tap **add field**.

The Add Field dialog box opens.

⑤ Tap a new field to add to the contact.

The Add Field dialog box closes, and the new field is added to the contact in the Info screen.

⑥ Type the information into the new field.

⑦ Tap **Done**.

Your iPad saves the new field for the contact and returns you to the All Contacts screen.

⑧ Repeat steps **2** to **7** to add fields for other existing contacts if needed.

Can I add a new field to a new contact?

Yes. But you need to type information into the empty fields before Contacts saves the new field. Follow these steps:

① Tap the **Plus** button (+) on the contacts page.

② Repeat steps **2** to **7** in this section.

What other types of fields can I add?

You can choose from 11 hidden fields: Prefix, Phonetic First Name, Phonetic Last Name, Middle, Suffix, Nickname, Job Title, Department, Instant Message, Birthday, and Date. The Birthday and Date fields can help you make sure that you do not miss birthdays or anniversaries.

Add Notes to a Contact

Sometimes, when you are adding an individual to your contacts list, it is very helpful to jot down some extra information about that person, such as where you met him or her, or the highlights of a recent meeting. Your iPad makes it easy for you to save important information such as this by enabling you to add notes to contacts.

① Tap **Contacts** on the Home screen.

The Contacts app opens.

② Tap the contact to which you want to add notes.

The contact's Info screen appears.

③ Tap **Edit**.

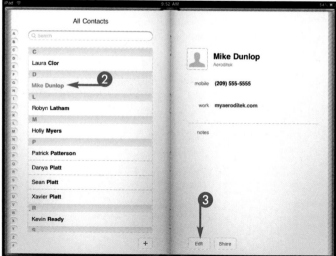

The Info screen appears.

4 Scroll down and then tap in the Notes field.

The on-screen keyboard appears.

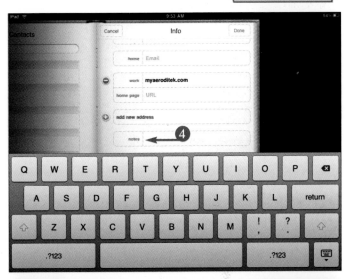

5 Type your notes.

6 Tap **Done**.

Your iPad saves the notes for the contact and returns you to the All Contacts screen.

Note: *You can tap the red button (⊖) that appears next to the note field in the Info screen to delete the notes if needed.*

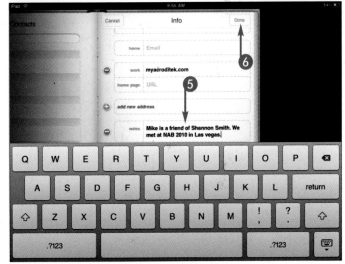

What are some other reasons for using notes?
Notes are great for quickly catching you up on extraneous information that may prove important to future interactions with that person. Perhaps you have met this person only once and were introduced by a fellow colleague. It may prove important in a future discussion to remember you share a mutual friend or acquaintance.

Add Photos to Contacts

Your iPad provides you with a surefire way not to forget the faces of important contacts by enabling you to add a personal photo to a contact. Because this version of iPad does not have the ability to take photos, you can sync a photo of a friend or colleague from your computer or use the camera connection kit to get photos onto your iPad. You can also download a photo from a webpage or an email. Adding a photo to a contact is quite easy and convenient.

Follow these steps with the Contacts app open.

① Tap the contact for which you want to add a photo.

The contact's information appears.

② Tap **Edit**.

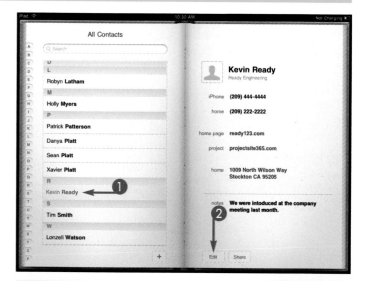

The Info screen appears.

③ Tap **add photo**.

Your iPad displays your photo albums.

④ Tap the photo album that contains the picture you want to add.

The photo album opens.

⑤ Tap the photo that you want to use.

The photo enlarges in the Choose Photo dialog box.

⑥ Move and scale the image so it looks the way you want in the contact.

Note: You can pinch and then open or close your fingers to increase or decrease the scale of the picture. You can also reposition the photo with your finger.

⑦ Tap **Use**.

The photo is inserted into the contact in the Info screen.

⑧ Tap **Done**.

Your iPad saves the photo with the contact and returns you to the All Contacts screen.

Can I assign a photo to a contact from the Photos app?
Yes. After you choose the collection of photos from which you want to choose the photograph, you can tap the Share button (icon) located in the upper-right corner of the screen to reveal the Assign to Contact option. Once you tap Assign to Contact, your list of contacts appears. Just tap a contact to assign the photograph.

Email Photo

Assign to Contact

Use as Wallpaper

Copy Photo

Add Appointments to Your Calendar

Your iPad was designed for you to be mobile while still enabling you to manage the important stuff, such as doctor appointments, business meetings, and anniversaries. The Calendar app can help to ensure that you do not overlook important event dates by enabling you to add them to calendars.

Note: *Follow these steps after you have already tapped Calendar on the Home screen and opened the Calendar app.*

1 Tap **Month**.

2 Use the arrows to navigate to the month of the event.

3 Double-tap the date on the calendar on which the event is to occur.

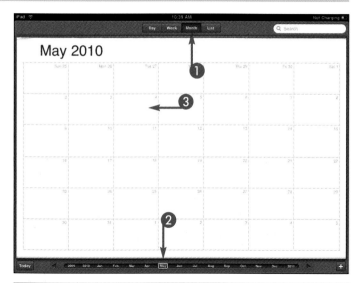

The Date opens in Day view.

4 Tap the **Plus** button ( ) in the bottom-right corner of the screen.

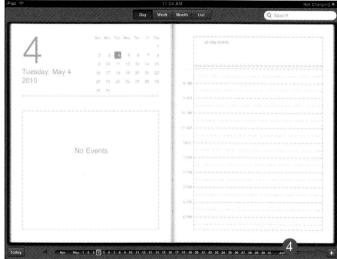

The Add Event dialog box opens.

The Title field contains a blinking cursor.

5 Type the title for the appointment.

Note: You can also choose to tap in the Location field to designate a location for the event.

The Start & End dialog box opens.

6 Tap **Starts**.

7 Use the scroll wheels to set the date and time the appointment begins.

8 Tap **Ends**.

9 Use the scroll wheels to set the date and time the appointment ends.

10 Tap **Done**.

Your iPad saves the data and returns you to the Add Event dialog box.

11 Tap **Done** in the Add Event dialog box.

The data is stored as an event, and your iPad returns to the Calendar screen. A dot appears under the date in the calendar to signify the Event. iPad lists all the events for that day at the bottom of the Calendar screen.

 TIP

How do I view the duration of the event for a particular date?

If you are unsure of how long you previously scheduled an event to last, you can follow these steps:

1 Tap the date in the calendar.

2 Tap **Day** to display a screen with the day, the date, the title of the appointment, and the duration of the event in blocks of time.

Edit an Existing Appointment

The details of your appointment, such as date and time, are always subject to change. Your iPad makes it easy for you to update your appointment schedules so your information is always up to date.

Edit an Existing Appointment

1 Tap **Calendar** on the Home screen.

The Calendar app opens.

2 Tap **Month**.

3 Use the arrows to navigate to the month of the event you want to edit.

4 Tap the date of the event you want to edit.

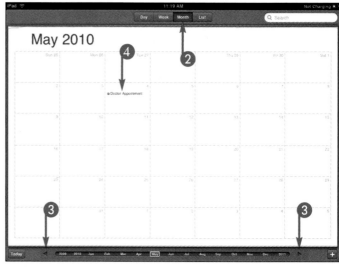

May 2010

A banner appears on screen for the event.

⑤ Tap **Edit**.

The **Edit Event** dialog box opens.

⑥ Make your changes to the appointment.

Note: *In this example, I have changed the end time for the event from 6 p.m. to 5 p.m.*

⑦ Tap **Done**.

Your iPad saves the data and returns you to the Event screen.

TIPS

Is there a way for me to view all the appointments I have made?

Yes. You can tap **List** in the Calendar view to view all the appointments you have entered into the calendar. Appointments are listed in the order in which they occur. This is a quick way for you to view the details of an appointment.

Can I follow these instructions for editing an event in a view other than Month?

Yes. You can edit an existing appointment in Week view, Day view, and List views. Note that in List view, you would first tap the name of the event on the left of the screen and then tap the actual event on the right to access the Edit Event box. In list view, there is no banner with an edit option. The Edit Event dialog box simply opens when you tap the event.

Set Up a Repeating Event

For those events that may occur routinely, Calendar enables you to enter the event one time and then schedule it to repeat at a regular interval. For example, if you want to schedule to meet a friend for lunch every day for a week while he or she is in town for business, you can create the event and schedule it to end in a week.

Lunch w/Jon
13th each month
12:00

Set Up a Repeating Event

① Tap the date for the repeating event.

A banner appears for the event.

② Tap **Edit** on the banner.

The Edit Event dialog box opens.

③ Tap **Repeat**.

The **Repeat Event** dialog box opens.

④ Tap the repeat interval you want.

⑤ Tap **Done**.

Calendar returns you to the Edit Event box.

6 Tap **End Repeat**.

The **End Repeat** dialog box opens.

7 Use the scroll wheels to set the date you want the repeated event to end.

8 Tap **Done**.

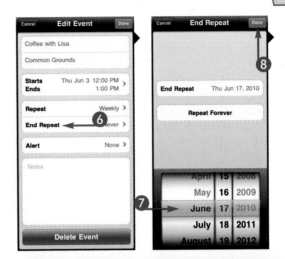

Your iPad saves the data and returns you to the Edit Event screen.

9 Tap **Done**.

The repeat data is saved.

TIPS

Can I set an event to repeat indefinitely?

Yes. You can choose for the event to repeat indefinitely by choosing **Repeat Forever** in step **7**. If you should want this event to end, you have to manually edit the End setting for the repeated event.

Can I add comments to my events?

Yes. Calendar enables you to add notes to an existing event from the Edit screen. You can tap in the Notes field of the Edit Event or Add Event dialog box to add details about the event or helpful reminders to help you manage your scheduled appointment.

Convert an Event to an All-Day Event

Sometimes, the events that you schedule may not have clear start and end times. In these circumstances, you may need to block out an entire day for an important activity. Calendar makes it easy for you to convert an event that you had previously scheduled for just an hour or two to an all-day event.

October 12
Seminars

"Defining Your Demographic"

① Tap the date for the event.

A banner appears for the event.

② Tap **Edit** on the banner.

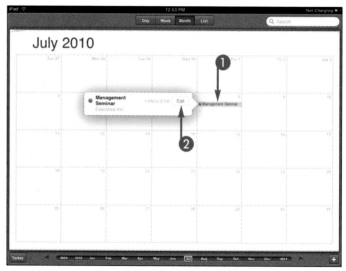

The Edit Event dialog box opens.

③ Tap **Starts**.

The Start & End dialog box opens.

④ Tap the **All-day** option to the **On** position.

⑤ Tap **Done**.

Calendar returns you to the Edit Event dialog box.

⑥ Tap **Done**.

The event is saved as an all-day event.

TIP

Are their any benefits to converting an event to all day rather than marking it to last from 9 to 5?

One benefit is that it provides an easier way to view a calendar by Day. If you specify that an event lasts from 9 a.m. to 5 p.m. and then schedule other appointments between that time, Calendar displays the blocks of time on top of one another in the Day view, which makes the schedule hard to read. All-day events are shown separately.

Add an Alert to an Event

Adding an alert to an event is a great way to give yourself a little reminder before the event takes place. You can use Calendar to send you an alert minutes, hours, or days before the event, and you can even set up more than one — just to be safe.

① Tap the date for the event.

A banner appears for the event.

② Tap **Edit** on the banner.

The Edit Event dialog box opens.

③ Tap **Alert**.

The Event Alert dialog box opens.

4 Tap the amount of time before the event that you want to receive the alert.

5 Tap **Done**.

Your iPad returns you to the Edit Event dialog box.

6 Tap **Done**.

Calendar saves the alert.

TIP

Is there any way that I can set up a backup alert?

Yes. You can set up a backup alert from the **Edit Event** dialog box before tapping **Done** in step **6** by tapping **Second Alert**. A backup alert can act as a failsafe to ensure that you do not miss an event, even if you are preoccupied. If you scheduled an alert a day before the event, you can set up a second alert two hours before — just to be sure.

Simplifying Your Life with the iPad

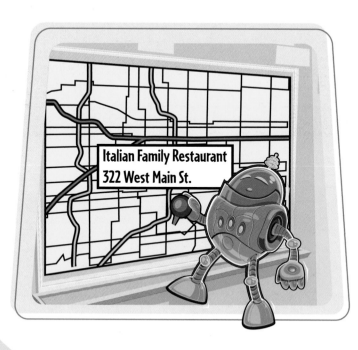

Italian Family Restaurant
322 West Main St.

Your iPad offers many tools that can help you simplify your life. Along with its many entertainment features, including media player capabilities, your iPad is also a personal digital assistant. iPad can also increase your productivity by helping you find the location of a hotel by using iPad's GPS capabilities, syncing with your MobileMe account, and running the Apple iWork suite of apps. In this chapter, you learn how to set up your iPad so you can take advantage of its many productivity features.

**Explore Accessibility Options for the
Visually and Hearing Impaired**................208

**Display Your Current Location
by Using Maps**.....................................210

Get Directions by Using Maps.....................211

**Specify a Location When You Do Not
Have an Address**..................................212

Display a Contact's Location.......................214

Bookmark a Location...................................216

Learn about MobileMe.................................218

**Set Up a MobileMe Account on
Your iPad**..220

**Configure MobileMe Synchronization
on the iPad**...222

**Configure MobileMe Synchronization
on Your Mac**...224

Set Up MobileMe on Your PC.......................226

Send Photos to Your MobileMe Gallery....228

Explore iWork...230

Explore Accessibility Options for the Visually and Hearing Impaired

The iPad possesses a feature that makes it more accommodating for individuals who may be visually impaired, hard of hearing, or deaf or who may have a physical or learning disability. The iPad is equipped with a screen reader and support for playback of closed-captioned content and other helpful universal access features. The accessibility options can be accessed by tapping **Settings** on the Home screen and then tapping the **General** option.

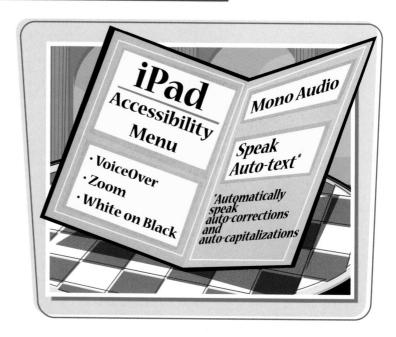

iPad Accessibility Menu

· VoiceOver
· Zoom
· White on Black

Mono Audio

Speak Auto-text*

*Automatically speak auto-corrections and auto-capitalizations

Enlarging the Screen

The iPad makes it easy for you to magnify the entire screen within any app so you can read content more clearly. You have the ability to zoom up to five times the normal size while panning the page left or right or up or down to get a closer look at a specific area on-screen. The Zoom feature can be found by tapping **Settings** on the Home screen and then tapping the **General** option. The Zoom feature also works in apps that you download from the App Store. If you require a higher contrast screen, your iPad enables you to change the display to white on black in any app.

Exploring Closed Captioning

Many of the movies and podcasts that you download from iTunes support closed captioning for the deaf and hearing impaired. Your iPad can display subtitles and closed captioning for supporting movies and podcasts. You can search for closed-captioned movies on iTunes and then download them directly to your iPad or Mac or PC.

The Monarch butterfly appears every spring, the best known of all butterflies.

Exploring VoiceOver

The iPad uses a VoiceOver feature that enables you to simply hold your finger against the screen and hear a description of the item under your finger. To select an item, you double-tap it and then flick three fingers to scroll. The VoiceOver feature utilizes 21 languages and lets you control the speaking rate. VoiceOver works with all the default apps installed on your iPad. A good thing to note here is that Apple has made it possible for software developers to create new apps that support the VoiceOver feature.

Exploring Mono Audio

If you are hard of hearing in one ear, iPad enables you to play both the right and left audio channels through both headphones. This allows you to hear both channels in either ear at a given time. The Mono Audio feature offers the convenience of enabling you to enjoy full sound through one earpiece.

Exploring Quick Access to Options

Regardless of which accessibility options you use the most, the iPad enables you to access them more quickly by providing the triple-click Home feature. You can configure your iPad to turn the VoiceOver, Zoom, or White on Black features off or on when you triple-click the Home button (▣). This saves you a trip from going into Settings each time you want to turn on or off one of these features.

Display Your Current Location by Using Maps

The Maps app can help you pinpoint your exact location if you should ever find yourself in an unfamiliar location. You can simply tap **Maps** on the Home screen and then tap the **Tracking** button to have Maps show your precise current location. The location is represented by a blue dot on a detailed map. You can use the map to find another location or just to know where you are in relation to other destinations.

Display Your Current Location by Using Maps

① Tap the **Tracking** button (◎) within the Maps app.

Maps asks if it is OK to use your current location.

② Tap **OK**.

● Maps drops a blue pushpin on your current location.

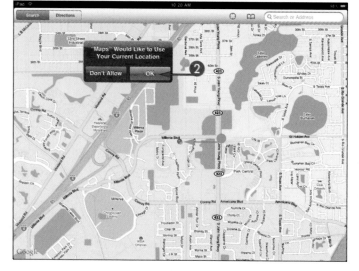

The Maps app can help you get from point A to point B by providing you accurate directions. You can get step-by-step driving or walking directions to a specified destination by typing the addresses for the starting location and the desired destination. You can also get directions for locations listed in your Contacts list by tapping your friend's name into the destination field instead of an actual address.

Get Directions by Using Maps

① Tap **Directions** in the Maps app.

The Start and End fields appear in the upper right, and the on-screen keyboard appears.

② Type the starting address into the Start field.

③ Type the destination in the End field.

Maps places a pushpin in the map for the start location.

Note: Notice that a Recents list appears, which displays a list of recent locations you have specified. If the location you want appears in the list, you can tap it to enter it into the field.

④ Tap **Search**.

Maps provides directions at the bottom of the screen.

Note: You can choose to receive driving, public transit, or walking directions.

Specify a Location When You Do Not Have an Address

The Maps app can also help you find locations for which you do not have an address. For example, you may know that a specific restaurant is located downtown, but you do not know how to get to downtown from your hotel. The Maps app enables you to add a pushpin where downtown is located on the map and then generate directions on how to get there.

Specify a Location When You Do Not Have an Address

1 Display the map of the city for which you want to specify a location.

Note: If you are currently in the city, you can tap the **Tracking** button (🜂) to display the city you want.

Note: You can also tap **Search** and then type the name of the city you need.

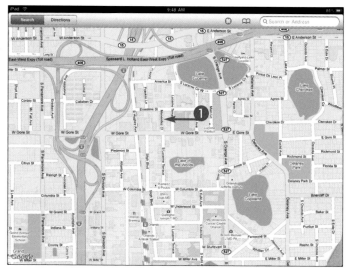

2 Pan and zoom the map with your finger to pinpoint the area you want to specify.

3 Tap the part of the screen that looks like a page curl in the bottom-right corner of the screen.

The page curls, revealing the Map, Overlays, and Drop Pin settings.

④ Tap **Drop Pin**.

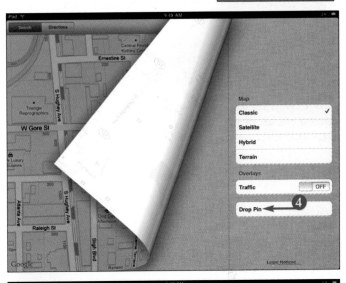

The Maps app drops a purple pushpin in the area you specified on the map.

⑤ Drag the purple pushpin to the location you want to specify on the map.

*Note: You can now tap **Directions** and then type the address for your current location and add the specified location to the End field.*

TIP

How do I find my way back from the specified destination to my original starting point?

You can find your way back to your original starting point by having your iPad reverse the directions for you. Tap the **Switch Start and End** button (⑤) located between the Start field and the End field under the Directions tab. The iPad reverses the directions so you can follow them back to your original destination. As with the previous directions, you can select directions for driving, public transit, and walking.

7901 santa monica ... ⑤ st hollywood, ca 90069 ⊗

Display
a Contact's Location

Both the Contacts and the Maps apps enable you to display a map of a contact's location. Simply tap a contact's physical address in the Contacts list to display a detailed map with streets named and the destination marked with a pushpin.

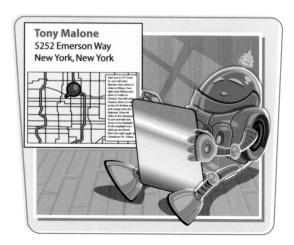

Display a Contact's Location

① Tap **Contacts** on the Home screen.

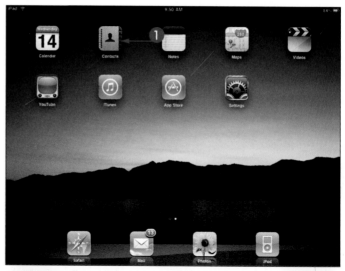

The Contacts app opens.

② Tap the contact that you want.

The contact data appears.

③ Tap the address that you want to map.

● The Maps app opens, displaying the contact's location.

④ Tap **Directions**.

⑤ Type your current address in the Start field.

Note: If you tap in the field, you can choose an address from the Recents list that appears.

⑥ Type the contact's address in the **End** field.

⑦ Tap **Search**.

Maps provides you with directions to that location.

TIP

Can I display a map of the contact's location starting within the Maps app?

Yes. You can view a contact's location from within the Maps app by following these steps:

① Tap **Maps** on the Home screen.

② Tap **Search**.

③ Tap the **Bookmarks** icon (📖).

④ Tap **Contacts**.

⑤ Tap a contact in the list.

Bookmark a Location

Typing the address for a destination that you do not visit often may not be a hassle, but having to do so continuously for locations that you frequently visit can get old. The Maps app can help with this. You can bookmark your most frequently used locations so you can quickly and easily retrieve directions. Saving locations as bookmarks helps you avoid typing addresses for which you frequently need directions.

Bookmark a Location

① Tap **Maps** on the Home screen.

The Maps app opens.

② Tap **Search**.

③ Type an address in the Search field.

④ Tap **Search**.

● The location is marked with a pushpin.

⑤ Tap the **Info** icon (ⓘ) to reveal details about the locations.

⑥ Tap **Add to Bookmarks**.

⑦ Modify the name of the bookmark if needed.

⑧ Tap **Save**.

Maps saves a bookmark of the location.

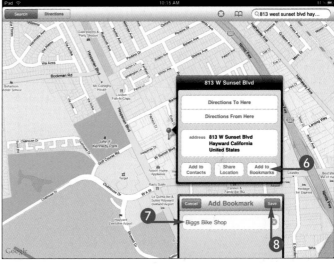

TIP

What if forgot to bookmark a location but need to find directions quickly?

You can search in the Recents list. Under Bookmarks is also a tab labeled Recents, which contains previous directions you have generated in the Maps app. Check to see if the search you need appears in the list. If so, you can simply tap the address in the list, and your iPad can show you where it is on the map as well as generate directions on how to get there.

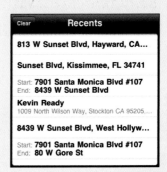

Learn about MobileMe

MobileMe is an Apple service that enables you to sync your email, contacts, and calendar events to multiple devices, such as your iPad, iPhone, Mac, and PC. Your MobileMe account also enables you to publish photos that can be shared with friends and family in your MobileMe Gallery. A MobileMe account requires a basic membership fee of $99 a year, and you can read more about it and sign up at www.apple.com/mobileme.

Syncing Mail, Contacts, and Calendar Events

A MobileMe account offers a very simple way to organize your life online. MobileMe makes it easy for you to access data, such as your mail, contacts, and calendar event information, on multiple devices by storing it in what Apple refers to as a cloud, which amounts to networked servers. Whenever you log in to your MobileMe account, you are able to access and manipulate your data by using an online interface that you can easily access from your iPad, iPhone, iPod touch, Mac, or PC.

Publishing to Your MobileMe Gallery

When you have a MobileMe account, you can upload photos from your iPad, iPhone, Mac, or PC so you can share them. A MobileMe Gallery enables friends and family to actively participate in the sharing of photos by downloading your photos or uploading their own. A MobileMe Gallery is a great way to showcase your favorite photos in a crisp, vibrant display.

Discovering MobileMe iDisk

Along with your MobileMe account, you also have access to what is called iDisk, which is essentially a personal hard drive you can access on the web. You can access your iDisk by logging in at www.me.com, where you can upload, download, and organize files to your iDisk, just like you would any other hard disk drive. The advantage of using your iDisk is that you can access it online from anywhere.

Finding a Lost iPod or iPhone

Your MobileMe account also comes with some helpful features you can use just in case you lose your iPad or iPhone. You can activate the Find My iPad feature in the MobileMe Settings on your iPad so that when you log in to www.me.com, you can log in to Find My iPad and display its location on a map. You also have the ability to remotely passcode-lock your iPad until it is found so no one can access your personal data.

Set Up a MobileMe Account on Your iPad

After you have signed up for a MobileMe account, you can easily configure your iPad to work with the account. Setting up your MobileMe account on your iPhone gives you the advantage of the many features MobileMe has to offer.

Set Up a MobileMe Account on Your iPad

① Tap **Settings** on the Home screen.

The Settings screen appears.

② Tap **Mail, Contacts, Calendars**.

The Mail, Contacts, Calendars screen appears.

③ Tap **Add Account**.

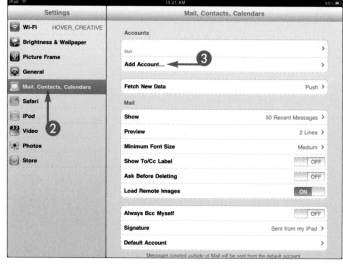

The Add Account screen appears.

4 Tap **MobileMe**.

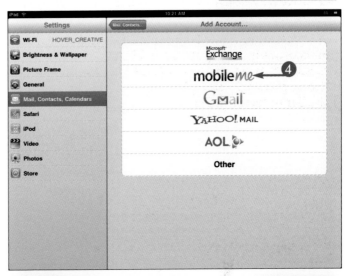

The MobileMe setup screen appears.

5 Type your name in the Name field.

6 Type your MobileMe email address in the Address field.

7 Type your MobileMe password in the Password field.

8 Tap **Next**.

MobileMe verifies the data you typed, and you are taken to a second screen.

9 Tap **Save**.

Note: *You can configure your MobileMe account to push — or automatically deliver — new data to your iPad when new information is available for Contacts or Bookmarks by tapping these options to the On position.*

Once I sign up for an account and set up MobileMe on my iPad, is my account ready to sync to all my devices?

No. You still have to inform your cloud about all the other devices you will be using. You have to configure each device — your iPhone, Mac, or PC — with your MobileMe account before your information is synced to all devices. Once each device is properly configured, you will be able to update information, such as a contact, with one device; the information is then sent to the cloud and updated for all the other devices.

Configure MobileMe Synchronization on the iPad

Your MobileMe account ensures that whenever new information is available for your email messages, contacts, and calendar events, it will be pushed to your iPad and other configured devices as soon as it is available. This keeps all your devices in sync. You can control the frequency in which new information is pushed to your iPad or decide to turn push off altogether on your iPad. Configuring MobileMe synchronization on your iPad enables you to control how you receive new information.

Configure MobileMe Synchronization on the iPad

① Tap **Settings** on the Home screen.

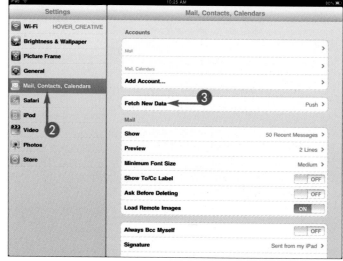

The Settings screen appears.

② Tap **Mail, Contacts, Calendars**.

The Mail, Contacts, Calendars screen appears.

③ Tap **Fetch New Data**.

The Fetch New Data screen appears.

④ Tap **Push** to the **Off** position if you do not want new information pushed to your iPad.

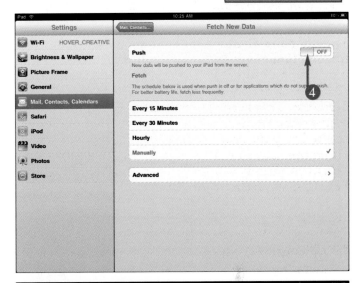

⑤ Tap the frequency with which your iPad will fetch new data.

● A check mark appears next to the chosen frequency.

TIP

What if my iPad has an app that does not support push?

When you tap the Push setting to the Off position or if your iPad contains an app that does not support Push, you can choose a schedule for when iPad fetches data. To conserve battery power, you should consider configuring your iPad to check for new information manually. You can also configure your iPad to check for new emails less frequently by choosing **Every 30 Minutes** or **Hourly**.

Configure MobileMe Synchronization on Your Mac

After you have signed up for a MobileMe account, configuring your Mac for synchronization is a very straightforward process. You can choose to sync your bookmarks, calendars, contacts, and mail accounts with the system preferences so that your information is always up to date on your devices. Make sure that you have the latest version of iTunes.

Configure MobileMe Synchronization on Your Mac

① Click the Apple on the main menu bar.

② Click **System Preferences**.

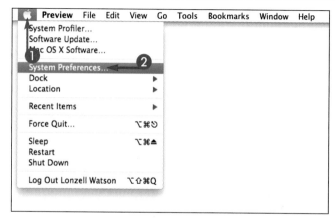

The System Preferences window opens.

③ Click **MobileMe**.

The MobileMe preference pane opens.

④ Click the **Sync** tab.

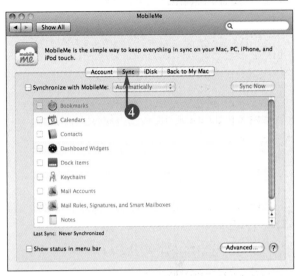

The sync options appear.

⑤ Click the **Synchronize with MobileMe** check box (☐ changes to ☑) and then choose **Automatically**.

⑥ Click the **Bookmarks** check box (☐ changes to ☑).

⑦ Click the **Calendars** check box (☐ changes to ☑).

⑧ Click the **Contacts** check box (☐ changes to ☑).

⑨ Click the **Mail Accounts** check box (☐ changes to ☑).

⑩ Click **Sync Now**.

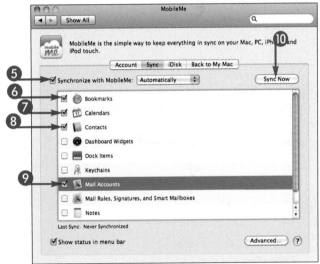

How do I access my iDisk on my Mac?

You can access your MobileMe iDisk by opening any Finder window. You can drag and drop files to save them on your iDisk and manage folders — just as any other hard disk drive. You also have the ability to locate another MobileMe member's iDisk or Public folder by using the Finder. You can password-protect your iDisk from the MobileMe preferences and give only select users the ability to read and write files to your personal iDisk.

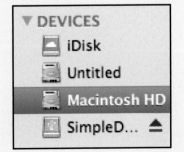

Set Up MobileMe on Your PC

After you have signed up for a MobileMe account, configuring your PC for synchronization is a very straightforward process. You can choose to sync your bookmarks, calendars, contacts, and mail accounts with the system preferences so your information is always up to date on your devices. Make sure you have the latest version of iTunes and that you have downloaded the latest version of MobileMe Control Panel for Windows.

Set Up MobileMe on Your PC

① Click the **Start** menu.

② Click **Control Panel**.

The Control Panel opens.

③ Click **Network and Internet Connections**.

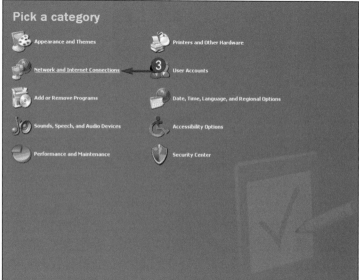

The Network and Internet Connection options appear.

④ Click **MobileMe**.

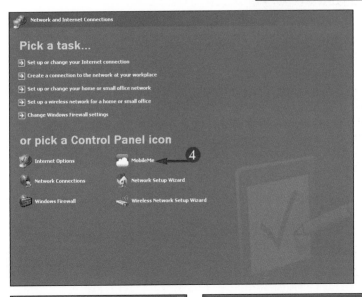

The MobileMe Sign In dialog box opens.

⑤ Type your member name and password.

⑥ Click **Sign In**.

The MobileMe Preferences dialog box opens.

⑦ Click the **Sync** tab.

⑧ Click the **Sync with MobileMe** check box (☐ changes to ☑) and then choose **Automatically**.

⑨ Click the check boxes for **Contacts**, **Calendars**, and **Bookmarks** (☐ changes to ☑).

⑩ Click **Sync Now**.

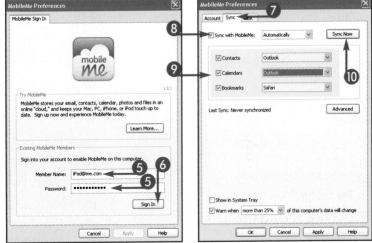

Can I review my MobileMe email messages with Outlook?

Yes. Keep in mind that you can always log in to your MobileMe account from your PC to check your email from a web browser if you do not want to set up your email client. If you want to set up your email client, you can go to the Tools menu in Outlook and then choose **E-mail Accounts** to access the Accounts Wizard and set up MobileMe email in Outlook.

Send Photos to Your MobileMe Gallery

Your iPad enables you to publish photos directly to your MobileMe Gallery. The MobileMe Gallery enables friends and family to actively participate in the sharing of photos by downloading your photos or uploading their own. If you do not have a MobileMe account, you can go to www.me.com to read more about it and to sign up.

Send Photos to Your MobileMe Gallery

① In the Photos app, tap the group of photos that contains the photo you want to publish.

② Tap the photo you want to publish.

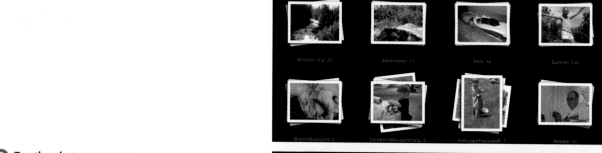

The photo fills the screen.

③ Tap the **Share** button ().

④ Tap **Send to MobileMe**.

The Publish Photo screen opens.

⑤ Type a title for the picture.

⑥ Type a description.

⑦ Tap **Publish**.

The photo is published to MobileMe.

Note: A dialog box opens, allowing you to view the photo you just published, tell a friend, or close the box.

How do I view my MobileMe Gallery without having published something?

After you publish a picture from your iPad to your MobileMe Gallery, you are given the opportunity to visit the gallery with just a single tap of a button. You may want to visit your site without having posted something first. Because your MobileMe account exists in an online cloud, you can access it from any browser. All you need to know is your gallery's web address, which usually appears like this: http://gallery.me.com/yourusername. To view a specific gallery, the web address looks more like this: http://gallery.me.com/yourusername/#gallery. Make sure that you write down and possibly bookmark the address of your galleries.

Explore iWork

iWork is Apple's productivity apps, which includes Keynote, Numbers, and Pages. Understanding the purpose of each piece of software in the suite can help you decide if iWork can make you more productive. These apps can be purchased separately for $9.99 each.

Explore Keynote

Keynote makes it easy for you to create high-quality, professional presentations with a tap of your finger. The Keynote app enables you to choose from professionally designed template themes to create your presentation. You can customize each presentation slide by swapping placeholder text and graphics with your own words and images. Choose from elements such as tables, charts, media, and shapes to add the finishing touches to your slides.

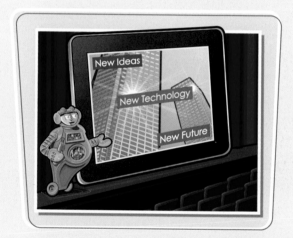

Explore Pages

Pages offers advanced tools for writing and easy page layout by using a collection of Apple-designed templates. You can use Pages to create high-quality résumés, brochures, schools reports, or invitations. Pages enables you to add tables and charts to display important data in your documents as well as copy data from other iWork apps, namely Numbers.

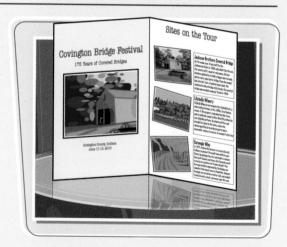

Explore Numbers

Numbers makes it easy for you to quickly create high-quality, attractive spreadsheets. Use the high-quality Apple-designed templates and easy-to-create formulas, tables, and charts to help you organize and plan. You can use Numbers to help you plan an event, save for retirement, track your diet, and even keep a journal.

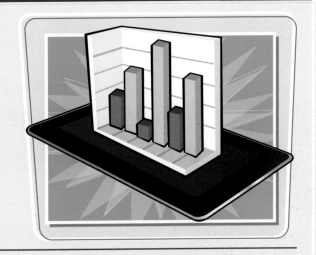

Purchase iWork for the iPad

Each iWork app has been redesigned for iPad so you can create professional presentations, word-processing documents, and spreadsheets with your fingertips. Each app is sold individually for $9.99 in the App Store, but you can also purchase the entire suite at once. The iWork apps are the most powerful productivity apps made for a mobile device, and they are easy to use.

Enhance Your iPad with the App Store

Although the iPad comes with some truly amazing apps right out of the box, you can expand its capabilities by downloading new apps from the App Store. You can choose from thousands of innovative apps, ranging from games to productivity apps. In this chapter, you learn how to search for apps, download from the App Store, move apps from your Mac or PC to your iPad, and keep your apps updated.

Explore the App Store **234**

Download Free Apps...**236**

**Purchase and Download Apps from
    the App Store**...**238**

**Move Apps from Your Computer
    to Your iPad**..**240**

Check for Updates to Apps **242**

Explore the App Store

Software developers from around the world have developed thousands of apps to take advantage of the iPad, iPhone, and iPod technologies. Apple has brought all these apps together in what is now known as the App Store, a virtual mall of software apps where expanding the capabilities of your iPad literally rests at your fingertips.

Accessing the App Store

You can access the App Store from your iPad by tapping the App Store icon or from your Mac or PC within the iTunes Store. Almost all the apps designed for the iPod touch and iPhone work with the iPad, so all you need to do is download them. You can also sync apps that you have previously downloaded for your iPhone or iPod touch to your iPad from your Mac or PC via the 30-pin dock connector.

Finding Apps in the App Store

Searching and downloading apps in the App Store is very similar to browsing for songs and albums in the iTunes Store. Once you tap the App Store icon, you can sort through content in a variety of ways, including Featured, Categories, Top 25, and Search. Choosing Featured lists the hot, new apps in the App Store, whereas Categories provides a more comprehensive search for apps. Use Categories to search content in collections such as Games, Social Networking, and Music. Top 25 lists the 25 most popular apps. You can also perform a keyword search.

Reading and Posting Reviews for Apps

There are tens of thousands of apps that you can download to your iPad, so use your storage space carefully by reviewing apps before you download them. Reading descriptions and reviews is easy in the App Store. Tapping an app icon in the App Store immediately opens the app description, complete with screenshots from the app. The App Store uses a five-star rating system; tap in the rating fields to read customer reviews of the apps. You can post your own review for an app by tapping the Write a Review field located above the customer reviews.

Download Free Apps

You need to set up an iTunes account before you can download apps in the App Store. Once you have created an account, you can download apps with just a few taps of your finger.

Download Free Apps

① Tap **App Store** on the Home screen.

② Locate the app you want to download and then tap **Free**.

The Free icon changes to the Install icon.

3 Tap **Install App**.

The App Store asks you to type your iTunes account password.

4 Type your iTunes username and password.

5 Tap **OK**.

The App Store begins to download the app. An icon for the app appears on the Home screen, along with a progress bar that tracks the download. The icon changes from loading to installing.

Note: When the download is complete, loading changes to the name of the app.

The app launches.

Can I play games on my computer that I downloaded from the App Store for the iPad?

No. The games and apps that you download from the App Store can be played only on your iPad, iPhone, and iPod touch. There may also be some apps made for the iPhone that may not be compatible with the iPad. Make sure that you carefully read the app description.

Purchase and Download Apps from the App Store

The App Store has a wide variety of sophisticated apps, some of which you have to pay for. The process for purchasing and downloading apps is almost identical to downloading free apps from the App Store. All purchases are made through your iTunes account.

Purchase and Download Apps from the App Store

① Tap **App Store** on the Home screen.

② Locate the app you want to download and then tap the price.

The Price button changes to Buy App.

③ Tap **Buy App**.

The App Store asks you to type your iTunes account password.

④ Type your iTunes username and password.

⑤ Tap **OK**.

The App Store begins to download the app. An icon for the app appears on the Home screen, along with a progress bar that tracks the download. The icon changes from loading to installing.

TIPS

Will I be charged twice if I attempt to download an app that I had previously paid for?

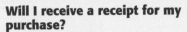

Usually not. When you attempt to download a previously purchased app, the App Store generally alerts you to this fact and asks if you would like to download it again for free. If you are rebilled for the second download, you can go to the app's information page located in the App Store and then tap **Report a Problem**.

Will I receive a receipt for my purchase?

Yes. The App Store emails you a copy of your receipt to the email address associated with your account. The process is not instantaneous, so it may take several days before you receive it. If you have made more than one purchase in a short period of time, you may receive a single receipt with several items listed. The App Store also sends you receipts for free downloads.

Move Apps from Your Computer to Your iPad

You can access the App Store in the iTunes Store under the App Store tab. You can sync the apps downloaded directly to your Mac or PC to your iPad.

Move Apps from Your Computer to Your iPad

① Connect your iPad to your computer.

② Launch iTunes.

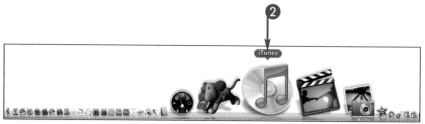

iTunes opens.

③ In iTunes, click **iPad** in the Devices list.

④ Click the **Apps** tab.

⑤ Click the **Sync Apps** check box (☐ changes to ☑).

⑥ Click the check boxes (☐ changes to ☑) next to the apps you want to sync.

Note: *You can also drag apps from the list on the left to the iPad Home screen on the right.*

Note: *If you have downloaded apps for an iPhone or iPod touch that are not iPad-compatible with your iPad, iTunes deselects the check boxes (☑ changes to ☐) for those apps in the list.*

⑦ Click **Apply**.

iTunes syncs the iPad with the apps you selected.

TIPS

Can I move apps off my iPad?

Yes. You can move apps off your iPad by deselecting the check box (☑ changes to ☐) next to the app in the list on the left. You can also navigate to the iPad Home screen on the right, roll the mouse pointer over the app you want to remove, and then click the ⊗ that appears in the upper-left corner. When you click Apply, the app is removed from the iPad.

Can I rearrange the apps on my iPad by using the iPad Home screen in iTunes?

Yes. You can drag app icons to rearrange them on the Home screen within iTunes. When you click **Apply**, the apps are rearranged on the iPad.

Check for Updates to Apps

The App Store notifies you when developers release a new version of an app that you have downloaded. You can perform updates from both your iPad and your computer. Updates are usually free.

Check for Updates to Apps

① Tap **App Store** on the Home screen.

Note: A number appears over the App Store button to signify how many apps installed on you iPad have available updates.

The App Store opens.

② Tap **Updates**.

The Updates screen appears with a list of all the apps that have available updates.

Note: You can access the update screen only if there are available updates for your downloaded apps.

③ Check for updates.

Note: *If all of your apps are up to date, nothing appears in the list. If updates are available for apps on your iPad, you can tap an update in the list to read a description of the update you have chosen.*

Note: *You can update one app at a time or you can choose to simply tap Update All to update all apps at once.*

④ Tap another category to browse more apps.

Can I update my apps from my computer?

Yes. You can update your downloaded apps from your Mac or PC by clicking Apps in the iTunes library. The icons for all the apps you have downloaded appear, with the number of updates available appearing in the bottom right corner. You can click **Updates Available** to download available updates.

Maintaining and Troubleshooting the iPad

Problems concerning the iPad software and hardware, including accessories, are quite rare. With that being said, there are a few fixes you can try if you should experience the occasional glitch that can occur with any hardware device. The good news is that although your iPad is an advanced piece of hardware, it is less complex than an actual computer, making any issue that may arise more manageable. In this chapter, you learn how to maintain your iPad and troubleshoot some common issues that may occur.

Update iPad Software...246

**Back Up and Restore Your iPad's
Data and Settings**...248

Learn to Extend Battery Life.........................250

Troubleshoot Connected Devices................252

**Troubleshoot the Inability to
Charge the iPad Battery**...............................254

**Troubleshoot Wi-Fi Problems with Wi-Fi
Accessibility**..256

**Troubleshoot Why iTunes May Not
See Your iPad**...258

**Troubleshoot the Inability to
Sync with iTunes**...260

Update iPad Software

Apple frequently releases software updates for the iPad operating system. Some updates fix security holes; others may add new features. To get the most from your iPad, it is good practice to sync your iPad regularly with iTunes and check if you are due for an update. Updating your iPad is a very straightforward process.

Update iPad Software

① Connect your iPad to your computer.

② Launch iTunes.

iTunes opens.

③ Click **iPad** in the Devices list.

④ Click the **Summary** tab.

A summary of your iPad appears.

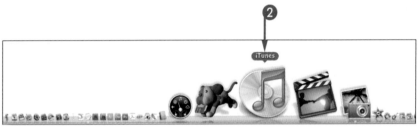

5 Click **Check for update**.

iTunes connects to Apple servers to check for an update. If an update is available, you see the iPad Software Update dialog box with a description of the update. If an update is not available, iTunes alerts you that the version of iPad software you are running is current.

6 Click **OK** if your iPad is up to date.

Note: *If your iPad is not up to date, you will have to click Next and then click Click Agree to accept the software agreement to begin the update.*

Note: *iTunes alerts you when the process is finished.*

Note: *If there is inadequate free space on your computer's hard drive, iTunes gives an alert and the backup is aborted.*

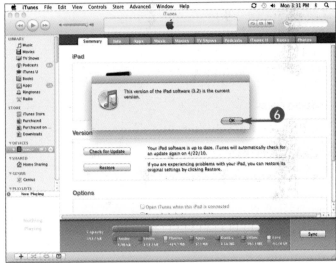

TIP

Does iTunes automatically check for updates each day?

No. Under the Summary tab in iTunes, in the field marked Version, iTunes gives you the date when it is scheduled to check for a new update. This is why you need to click the Check for Update button. There may be a new software update, but iTunes has not checked for it yet.

Back Up and Restore Your iPad's Data and Settings

Sometimes, the iPad may function sporadically or appear unstable if its settings should become corrupt. This is a very rare occurrence, but if it should happen, you should restore your iPad to the factory default settings. The Restore feature in iTunes enables you to back up your settings.

Back Up and Restore Your iPad's Data and Settings

① Connect your iPad to your computer.

② Launch iTunes.

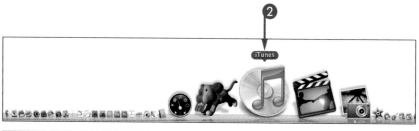

iTunes opens.

Note: *Your iPad must be visible to iTunes in order to perform these steps.*

③ Click **iPad** in the Devices list.

④ Click the **Summary** tab.

A summary of your iPad appears.

⑤ Click **Restore**.

iTunes asks if you want to back up
your settings.

*Note: Keep in mind that you need enough space
available on your computer hard disk for however
much is on your iPad.*

6 Click **Back Up**.

iTunes asks you to confirm if you
want to restore your iPad.

7 Click **Restore**.

**Is there any way that I can protect my
personal information while backing up
my data?**

Yes. When you back up your iPad data, any
sensitive materials you may have become part of
the backup files. If someone were so inclined, he
or she could review these files. You can protect
confidential files by clicking the **Encrypt iPad
Back Up** check box (☐ changes to ☑) and then
setting a decryption password under the Summary
tab in step **4**.

Open iTunes when this iPad is connected
Sync only checked songs and videos
Prefer standard definition videos
Convert higher bit rate songs to 128 kbps AAC
Manually manage music and videos
☑ Encrypt iPad backup   Change Password...
Configure Universal Access...

Learn to Extend Battery Life

The iPad is capable of up to ten hours of battery life, but battery life can vary depending on how you use the iPad. There are a few things you can do to extend the life of your iPad's battery.

Dim the Screen

The 9.7-inch multi-touch screen can drain plenty of battery power. The higher the brightness level you set for the screen, the more battery power your iPad consumes. Consider dimming the screen to extend the life of your battery. If you are viewing the screen in very bright conditions, you probably do not need a very high brightness setting.

Utilize Sleep Mode

When your iPad is awake, it is consuming battery power. You do not have wait for the iPad to go into Sleep mode automatically; you can manually put the iPad asleep. For example, if your iPad use is interrupted, such as by the arrival of a delivery person, press the Sleep button before setting it down. If you get into the habit of putting your iPad to sleep when you do not need its services, you will conserve battery power.

Turn Off Wi-Fi

When the Wi-Fi antenna is on, the iPad is constantly looking for available Wi-Fi networks to join, which uses battery power. If you do not require a Wi-Fi network, turn off the Wi-Fi antenna to conserve battery power. Tap the **Settings** icon on the Home screen and then tap **Wi-Fi** to put it into the **Off** position.

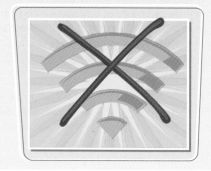

Turn Off Bluetooth

When the Bluetooth feature is set to the On position, it is constantly checking for Bluetooth devices with which to connect, which uses battery power. Consider turning off the Bluetooth feature when you are not using Bluetooth devices. You can tap **Settings** on the Home screen, tap **General**, and then turn off the Bluetooth setting.

Turn Off GPS

When the iPad GPS is on, the receiver exchanges data with the GPS system regularly and drains precious battery power. Consider turning off the GPS antenna when the GPS is not needed. Tap **Settings** on the Home screen, tap **General**, and then change the Location Services setting to off. GPS is available only for the 3G model iPads.

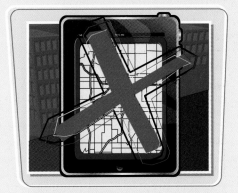

Avoid Extreme Temperatures

Extreme temperature — either hot or cold — has an effect on the performance of the battery and can even cause damage. Keep your iPad in a climate-controlled environment to maintain the long-term effectiveness of your battery.

Troubleshoot Connected Devices

You can connect devices to your iPad via a headset jack or a dock connector as well as Bluetooth. If you should have problems with any of these connection methods, you can try a few things to solve the issue.

Check Connections and Power Switches

The first thing you can do and perhaps the most elementary is to make sure your physical connections are secure and the power to your connected devices is on. If you are not used to turning on a second device, such as a headset, it is very easy to forget. Also, make sure your ports are clean. Lint and dirt can make it difficult for the connectors to secure themselves.

Replace Batteries

There is also a chance that the battery in your connected device may need to be replaced. If a device, such as a headset, is cutting in and out or does not work at all, try replacing the battery. Some wireless devices can really drain battery power.

Restart Devices

You can power-cycle the device in question, which means you can turn off the device and then turn it on again. When you turn off the device, leave it off for a few seconds to ensure that the insides of the device have actually powered down. If the device does not have an off and on switch, take the battery out. You would be surprised how often simply turning a device off and then turning it back on again can solve minor issues.

Reset Devices

It is possible that the device may have become confused because of a setting you have adjusted, which can happen when you configure a device. You can try resetting the device to its original factory settings to see if doing so fixes the issue.

Upgrade Firmware

Some devices use software to run their internal functions, called *firmware*. For example, routers and some video cameras have firmware. You can check with the manufacturer of the device to see if an upgrade is available for a particular device. A simple firmware upgrade may solve the issue.

Troubleshoot the Inability to Charge the iPad Battery

If you ever experience a problem where you cannot charge the iPad, you can try a few things to troubleshoot the issue. Understanding a few basic troubleshooting tips can help you decide if the problem is minor or if you may need to replace the battery.

Check Your Cable Connections

If your iPad does not charge, perhaps the first thing you should do is confirm that the cables are actually connected and secure. Make sure that the dock is attached firmly to the 60-pin connector at the bottom of the iPad and that the USB end is firmly attached to your computer or adapter. You also want to make sure that the connectors are free of any dirt or dust that may hinder the charge. A faulty adapter also will not supply power to the iPad. Make sure you try another wall socket or another power supply if you have one.

Switch USB Ports

If you are using your USB to Dock connector to connect to your computer, you can also try connecting to a different USB port. The USB port located on the keyboard may not transfer enough power to charge the iPad. If you are connected to this USB port, try disconnecting and connecting to a USB port located on the computer itself.

Wake Up Your Computer

Some computers do not charge the iPad when they are asleep; others do. If your computer does not charge the iPad when its asleep, you can simply wake it up and configure your computer not to sleep while you are charging the iPad.

Set Up a Service Appointment

If you still cannot charge the iPad, it is entirely possible that you may need to replace the battery. One way to determine this is to schedule a service appointment at your local Apple Store or ship the iPad to Apple for inspection. Receiving technical support or setting up a service appointment is made very simple when you go to Apple.com.

Service
Diploma
Dr. Apple
cellent Technical Support

Troubleshoot Wi-Fi Problems with Wi-Fi Accessibility

iPad provides you with the flexibility and convenience of wireless networking via Wi-Fi connectivity. Along with this convenience comes the potential for accessibility issues. Understanding a few basic issues that may arise can help you troubleshoot Wi-Fi accessibility problems.

Make Sure the Wi-Fi Antenna Is On

First and foremost, make sure that the iPad Wi-Fi antenna is turned on. You can quickly determine if the Wi-Fi antenna is on by looking in the upper-left corner of iPad for the Wi-Fi icon. If it is not turned on, you can tap **Settings**, tap **Wi-Fi**, and then tap the Wi-Fi switch to **On**.

Turn Off Airplane Mode

You can quickly determine if iPad is in Airplane mode by looking in the upper-left corner of iPad for the airplane icon. You can tap **Settings** and then tap **Airplane Mode** to switch off this mode. You will need to turn Wi-Fi Off for your Wi-Fi model iPad.

Disconnect and Reconnect to the Network

Simply disconnecting and reconnecting to the network can solve some Wi-Fi problems. Tap **Settings**, tap **Wi-Fi**, tap the **More Info** icon for the Wi-Fi network to which you are connected, and then tap **Forget This Network** to disconnect. Try reconnecting to the same network.

Check Your Range

You can be only about 115 feet from a Wi-Fi access point before the signal becomes weak or drops altogether. You can either move closer to the access point to improve your connection or turn on the access point's range booster if it has one.

Reset Network Settings

You can try removing all stored network data on your iPad to try and solve a Wi-Fi accessibility issue. When you reset your iPad, you are essentially bringing it back to its factory state. Tap **Settings**, tap **Network Settings** to clear all stored network data, and then try reconnecting.

Reset Your Router

The issue may not rest with the iPad; you can try resetting the router to its factory state. Use this as a last resort because resetting your router means that you will have to set up your network again from the ground up.

Troubleshoot Why iTunes May Not See Your iPad

When you attach your iPad to your computer with the iTunes application running on your Mac or PC, iPad should show up in the Devices list. If it does not show in the Devices list, this means that iTunes does not recognize your iPad. You can try a few fixes to correct this problem.

Check Your Cable Connection

The first place you may want to start is to ensure that the cable to your iPad and your computer is connected securely. It can prove embarrassing to run through the entire litany of fixes, only to discover that the cables were not connected securely. You should also make sure that the ports and connector are free of dust and grime for a solid connection.

Restart Your iPad

You can try turning off your iPad and then turning it back on to see if that solves the problems. When you power-cycle your iPad, leave it off for a few seconds to ensure that the device has completely powered down. Turn the device on again to see if iTunes can now recognize your iPad.

Switch to Another USB Port

The USB port in which you have the iPad connected simply may not work. If you are using a port on a USB hub to connect your iPad, try removing it and connecting directly to a USB port located on the computer itself.

Restart the Computer

You can try restarting the computer on which you have iTunes to see if iTunes then recognizes your iPad. Restarting the computer resets the USB ports and may enable iTunes to recognize your iPad. It is a simple fix, but you would be surprised how often this basic troubleshooting tip fixes the problem.

Check the iPad Display

When connected to a computer, iPad usually gives you a message alerting you to what it is doing. Occasionally, you may see a message that reads "Charging...please wait." In this case, the iPad may have to charge a few minutes before it has sufficient battery power to operate. You may even see a message indicating that your iPad requires service.

Verify Your Computer Meets System Requirements

If your computer does not meet the system requirements for your iPad, you will experience problems. Your iPad requires Mac OS X v10.5.8 or later with iTunes 9.1 or later. On a PC, iPad requires Windows 7, Windows Vista, or Windows XP Home or Professional with Service Pack 3 or higher. iTunes 9.1 or later is also required for a PC.

Mac OS X v10.5.8 w/ iTunes 9.0

iPad w/ Windows 7, Windows Vista, Windows XP Home or Professional w/ Service Pack 3 w/ iTunes 9.0

Troubleshoot the Inability to Sync with iTunes

Without the ability to sync your iPad to your computer, you are unable to share data, such as your contacts and calendars, or music and videos with your Mac or PC. Here are some things you can try if iTunes recognizes but still does not sync your iPad.

Check File Format

If you are having problems syncing your music and videos with iTunes, confirm that the files are compatible with your iPad. Files such as WMA, MPEG-1, MPEG-2, and others are not readable by the iPad. You will need to convert these files to a format compatible with your iPad. Once the files have been converted, try syncing them again.

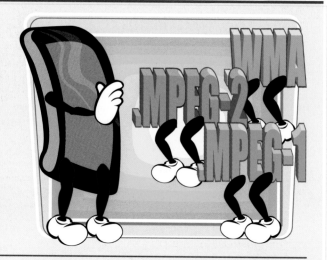

Solve Sync Conflicts

Whenever you edit information, such as in your contacts, on the iPhone, or on your computer, those edits are copied in the sync. iTunes can become confused if you make two different edits to the same information — one on your iPad; the other on your computer. For example, if you made a different edit to the same email address information on both the iPad and the computer, iTunes does not know which is the correct version. Before you can sync, you need to use Conflict Resolver.

Check Automatic Sync

If you connect your iPad to your computer and iTunes does not respond, iTunes may not be set to automatically sync. You can click **iPad** in the Devices list and then click the **Summary** tab to make sure that the **Automatically sync when this iPad is connected** check box is selected (☐ changes to ☑).

Check Free Space

If the available space on your iPad is exceeded by the space required for the content you want to sync, iTunes cannot perform the sync; a message usually alerts you about this. In order to avoid this issue, free up some space on your iPad to allow for the new content or choose to sync less content to your iPad. Before you begin the sync process, you can check the space needed for the sync in iTunes as well as check your available space on your iPad under Settings.

Index

Numerics

3G
  connecting to, 6
  managing data plan, 65
  monitoring data usage, 64
  overview, 4, 61
  roaming charges, 65
  signing up for, 64
30-pin connector, 5
802.11. *See* Wi-Fi

A

accessibility options
  closed captioning, 208
  enlarging screen, 208
  Mono Audio, 209
  overview, 12
  quick access to options, 209
  VoiceOver, 209
accessories
  camera connection kit, 6, 18, 31, 47, 130
  case, 30
  dock, 30
  keyboard dock, 6, 31, 75, 111
  overview, 6
  USB power adapter, 31
Account switch, 93
Accounts button, 91
Accounts screen, 91
Add Account screen, 84–85, 221
Add Bookmark option, 72
Add Event dialog box, Calendar app, 197
Add Field dialog box, Contacts app, 191
Add Mail Account screen, 86
add new address field, Contacts app, 187
Address field
  Add Account screen, 85
  New Account screen, 86
Airplane mode
  overview, 13
  turning on/off, 45, 256

AirPort. *See* Wi-Fi
albums, viewing, 18
All calendars radio button, iTunes, 117
All Contacts list, 77
app icons
  deleting, 35
  moving, 11, 34–35
App Store
  accessing, 234
  browsing, 26
  buying apps, 238–239
  finding apps, 235
  free apps, 236–237
  moving apps from computer to iPad, 240–241
  overview, 7, 26
  previously purchased apps, 239
  receipts for purchases, 239
  reviews for apps, 235
  updating, 27, 242–243
  video games, 26
appointments. *See also* Calendar app
  alerts, adding to events, 204–205
  converting events to all-day events, 202–203
  creating, 196–197
  editing, 198–199
  overview, 21
  repeating events, 200–201
  viewing all, 255
apps
  accessing, 234
  buying, 238–239
  finding, 235
  free, 236–237
  moving from computer to iPad, 240–241
  moving off iPad, 241
  rearranging, 241
  reviews for, 235
  syncing to iPad from Mac, 27
  updating, 27, 242–243
  video games, 26
AT&T, 64, 65
audio settings, 146–147

audiobooks
    choosing which to sync, 127
    managing manually, 127
    syncing, 126–127
authentication, configuring, 96–97
Authentication screen, 97
Authorize Computer option, iTunes, 141
Auto Lock screen, 41
Auto-Brightness setting, Brightness & Wallpaper screen, 44
AutoFill feature, 76–77
AutoFill option, Safari screen, 77
AutoFill screen, 77
Auto-Lock option, General screen, 40
Automatically sync when this iPad is connected check box, 261

B

backing up data and settings, 248–249
battery charging
    overview, 111
    troubleshooting, 254–255
battery life
    automatic email checking, 99
    Bluetooth, 251
    charging, 111
    dimming screen, 250
    disabling email addresses to conserve, 92
    extreme temperatures, 251
    GPS, 251
    overview, 6
    push accounts, 93
    Sleep mode, 41, 250
    Wi-Fi, 250
Bluetooth
    keyboards, 30
    overview, 6
    turning on/off, 251
bookmarking
    editing bookmarks, 73
    locations, 29, 216–217
    relevancy, 121
    RSS feeds, 79

syncing bookmarks, 73, 120–121
    websites, 72–73
Bookmarks check box, MobileMe Preferences, 225, 227
Bookmarks icon
    Safari, 73
    YouTube app, 169
books
    browsing iBooks, 172
    buying, 172, 174–175
    downloading previously purchased, 175
    overview, 6
    reading, 173
    settings, 173
Books tab, iTunes, 126
Brightness & Wallpaper option, Settings screen, 44
Brightness & Wallpaper screen, 44, 46
browser cache, clearing, 71
Buy Album button, iTunes, 141
Buy App button, App Store, 239
Buy Book button, iBooks, 175
Buy Single button, iTunes, 141
buying
    apps, 238–239
    books, 172, 174–175
    from iTunes, 24, 138, 140–141
    iWork suite, 23, 231

C

Calendar Alerts setting, Sounds screen, 42
Calendar app
    alerts, adding to events, 204–205
    backup alerts, 205
    comments, adding to events, 201
    converting events to all-day events, 202–203
    creating appointments, 196–197
    editing appointments, 198–199
    overview, 7, 21
    repeating events, 200–201
    syncing calendars, 116–117
    viewing all appointments, 199
    viewing duration of events, 197

Index

Calendars check box, MobileMe Preferences, 225, 227
camera, importing photos from
    downloading images, 135
    SD card reader, 135
    USB to Dock adapter, 134
camera connection kit, 6, 18, 31, 47, 130
cases, 30
Categories list, App Store, 235
Cellular Data option, Setting screen, 64
Cellular Data Plan window, 64
Cellular Data Roaming option, 65
Change Passcode Lock option, General screen, 39
Choose Photo dialog box, Contacts app, 195
Clipboard, 52
closed captioning, 208
Closed Captioning setting, Video options, 155
comments, YouTube, 165
configuring iPad
    Airplane mode, turning on/off, 45
    cutting, copying, and pasting
        editable text, 52–53
        non-editable text, 52
        photos, 54–55
    Home button, 43
    Home screen
        customizing, 34–35
        resetting default layout, 36–37
    parental controls, 48–49
    passcodes, 38–39
    resetting iPad, 50–51
    screen brightness, adjusting, 44
    searching using Spotlight, 56–57
    Sleep setting, 40–41
    sounds, turning on/off, 42
    wallpaper, 46–47
    Wi-Fi, turning on/off, 45
Conflict Resolver dialog box, 115
connected devices, troubleshooting
    checking connections and power switches, 252
    replacing batteries, 252
    resetting devices, 253
    restarting devices, 253
    upgrading firmware, 253

contacts
    adding fields for, 190–191
    assigning email addresses to, 182–183
    assigning photos to, 19, 194–195
    assigning physical addresses to, 186–187
    assigning web addresses to, 184–185
    creating, 178–179
    deleting, 179
    editing, 180–181
    emailing videos to, 171
    finding quickly, 181
    labels, 188–189
    notes, 192–193
    syncing, 114–115
Contacts app
    adding fields, 190–191
    assigning email addresses to contacts, 182–183
    assigning photos to contacts, 19, 194–195
    assigning physical addresses to contacts, 186–187
    assigning web addresses to contacts, 184–185
    creating contacts, 178–179
    deleting contacts, 179
    editing contacts, 180–181
    emailing videos to contacts, 171
    finding contacts quickly, 181
    labels, 188–189
    managing contacts, 21
    notes, 192–193
    overview, 7, 21
    syncing contacts, 114–115
    viewing contact location, 29, 214–215
Contacts check box, MobileMe Preferences, 225, 227
cookies, 71
Copy button, 52, 54
copying
    photos, 54–55
    text, 52–53, 75
Custom Label screen, Contacts app, 189
cutting
    editable text, 52–53
    non-editable text, 52

D

Day view, Calendar app, 196
Deauthorize Computer option, iTunes, 141
Default Account option, Mail, Contacts, Calendars screen, 88
Default Account Screen, 89
deleting
    app icons, 35
    contacts, 179
    email accounts, 83
    YouTube videos from Favorites category, 169
Description field
    Add Account screen, 85
    New Account screen, 86
Devices list, iPad not visible in, 258–259
Devices pane, iTunes, 113
Devices tab, iTunes, 113
directions, 28, 211
Directions option, Maps app, 211
disabling
    email accounts, 83, 92–93
    remote email message images, 106–107
display. See also multi-touch screen
    adjusting brightness of, 44, 250
    battery life, 6
    enlarging, 208
    overview, 4
Do not sync events older than 30 days check box, iTunes, 117
dock (for charging and syncing), 30
Dock (Home screen), moving icons to, 35
documents
    buying iWork suite, 23, 231
    Keynote app, 22, 230
    Numbers app, 23, 231
    Pages app, 22, 230
Drop Pin option, Maps app, 213

E

eBooks
    browsing iBooks, 172
    buying, 172, 174–175

downloading previously purchased, 175
overview, 6, 7
reading, 173
settings, 173
EDGE, 61
Edit Event dialog box, Calendar app, 199, 200, 202–203
802.11. See Wi-Fi
email
    accounts
        adding, 84–85
        creating, 86–87
        disabling, 92–93
        managing, 20, 82–83
        settings, 91
        specifying default, 88–89
        switching, 90–91
        syncing, 118–119, 139
    assigning addresses to contacts, 182–183
    authentication, configuring, 96–97
    automatically checking for messages, 98–99
    disabling remote message images, 106–107
    font size, 102–103
    Mail app
        connecting with services, 82
        deleting accounts, 83
        disabling accounts, 83
        overview, 20
        saving photos from attachments, 132
        setting up iPad-only accounts, 83
        specifying default account, 83
        switching accounts, 83
    overview, 17
    protocols, 83
    recognized services, 20, 82, 84
    reviewing with Outlook, 227
    saving photos from, 132–133
    security, 70
    sending links, 20, 100–101, 170–171
    sending photos, 19, 158–159
    server ports, switching, 94–95
    signatures, 20, 104–105
    storing on server, 87
    viewing, 20

Index

Email Photo option, Photos app, 159
Enable Restrictions option, Restrictions screen, 48
Encrypt iPad Back Up check box, 249
End Repeat dialog box, Calendar app, 201
Enhanced Data rates for GSM (Global System for Mobile Communication) Evolution, 61
EQ options, iPod app, 147
EQ setting, iPod app, 146
Erase All Content and Settings option, Reset screen, 51
eReader, 7. *See also* iBooks app
Event Alert dialog box, Calendar app, 205

F

favorites
    videos, 168–169
    websites, 72–73
Favorites category, YouTube, 166, 169
Featured category
    App Store, 235
    YouTube, 166
Fetch Data screen, 99
Fetch New Data option, Mail, Contacts, Calendars screen, 98, 222
Fetch New Data screen, 223
file formats, 131, 260
Find My iPad feature, 219
firmware, upgrading, 253
font size, email message, 102–103
Fraud Warning feature, 70
free apps, 236–237
Free button
    App Store, 236–237
    iTunes, 143
free space, 261
full-screen view, 6
full-sized keyboards, 30, 75, 135

G

games
    downloading, 26
    playing on computers, 237

General option, Settings screen, 36
Genius Mixes, 151
Genius Playlists, 151
gestures
    scrolling, 74
    tapping
        double-tapping, 74
        one tap, 74
        tapping, holding, and dragging, 75
    zooming, 74
Get Episode button, iTunes, 143
Google, 66
GPS, 251
groups, YouTube, 165

H

headphone jack, 5
History feature, Safari, 71
History option, YouTube, 167
Home button, 5, 8, 43
Home option, General screen, 43
Home screen
    customizing, 10, 34–35
    deleting icons from, 35
    resetting default layout, 36–37

I

iBooks app
    browsing, 172
    buying books, 172, 174–175
    downloading previously purchased books, 175
    overview, 6
    reading books, 173
    settings, 173
iDisk, 219, 225
IMAP (Internet Message Access Protocol), 83, 86, 87
importing photos
    downloading images, 135
    overview, 18
    SD card reader, 135
    USB to Dock adapter, 134

In-App Purchases setting, Restrictions screen, 49
Include music videos check box, iTunes, 123
Incoming Mail Server section, 87
Info icon, Maps app, 217
Info pane, iTunes, 114–116, 119–120
Install App button, App Store, 237
Internet
    3G
        connecting to, 6
        managing data plan, 65
        monitoring data usage, 64
        overview, 4, 61
        roaming charges, 65
        signing up for, 64
    assigning web address to contacts, 184–185
    bookmarking favorite websites, 72–73
    EDGE cellular technology, 61
    email
        account settings, 91
        adding accounts, 84–85
        assigning addresses to contacts, 182–183
        authentication, configuring, 96–97
        automatically checking for messages, 98–99
        connecting with services, 82
        creating accounts, 86–87
        deleting accounts, 83
        disabling accounts, 83, 92–93
        disabling remote message images, 106–107
        font size, 102–103
        managing accounts, 20, 82–83
        overview, 17
        protocols, 83
        recognized services, 20, 82, 84
        reviewing with Outlook, 227
        saving photos from, 132–133
        security, 70
        sending links, 20, 100–101, 170–171
        sending photos, 19, 158–159
        server ports, switching, 94–95
        setting up iPad-only accounts, 83
        signatures, 20, 104–105
        specifying default account, 83, 88–89
        storing on server, 87

        switching accounts, 83, 90–91
        syncing accounts, 118–119, 139
        viewing, 20
    Internet Service Providers, 60
    managing multiple browser pages, 17, 68–69
    Safari browser, 16
    search engines, changing default, 66–67
    security and privacy options
        clearing browser History and cache, 71
        cookies, 71
        Fraud Warning, 70
        JavaScript, 70
        pop-up blocking, 71
    Wi-Fi
        connecting to, 6, 62–63
        overview, 4, 60
        troubleshooting, 256–257
        turning on/off, 45, 250
Internet Message Access Protocol (IMAP), 83, 86, 87
Internet Service Providers (ISP), 60
iPad. *See also* accessories
    battery life, 6
    buttons, 5
    capabilities of
        appointments, 21
        apps, 26–27
        contacts, 21
        documents, 22–23
        email, 20
        Internet, 16–17
        maps, 28–29
        music and videos, 24–25
        notes, 21
        overview, 4
        photos, 18–19
    configuring, 34–57
        Airplane mode, turning on/off, 45
        cutting, copying, and pasting, 52–55
        Home button, 43
        Home screen, 34–37
        parental controls, 48–49
        passcodes, 38–39
        resetting, 50–51

Index

screen brightness, adjusting, 44
searching using Spotlight, 56–57
Sleep setting, 40–41
sounds, turning on/off, 42
wallpaper, 46–47
Wi-Fi, turning on/off, 45
connecting to computer, 110–111
connecting to Wi-Fi and 3G networks, 6
design of, 5
features of
    App Store, 7
    Calendar app, 7
    Contacts app, 7
    iBooks app, 7
    Maps app, 7
    Notes app, 7
    playing videos, 6
maintaining
    backing up and restoring data and settings,
      248–249
    battery life, 250–251
    updating software, 246–247
overview, 4
restarting, 258
selling, 13
settings
    accessibility options, 12
    Airplane mode, 13
    audio, 146–147
    parental controls, 12
    restoring default presets, 13
    video, 154–155
technical specifications, 4
iPhoto, 131
iPod app
accessing playback controls while using other apps, 149
audio settings, 146–147
browsing content, 148–149
overview, 24–25
playing content, 148–149, 152–153
playing music, 24
playlists, creating, 150–151
video settings, 154–155

iPod settings, 146
ISP (Internet Service Providers), 60
iTunes
    backup and restoration, 248–249
    buying content, 138, 140–141
    organizing content, 138
    playlists, 139
    podcasts, subscribing to, 142–143
    rating content in iTunes Store, 144–145
    recognition of iPad
      cable connection, 258
      checking display, 259
      restarting computer, 259
      restarting iPad, 258
      system requirements, 259
      USB ports, 258
    syncing
      apps, 240–241
      audiobooks, 126–127
      automatic, 261
      bookmarks, 120–121
      calendars, 116–117
      connecting iPad to computer, 110–111
      contacts list, 114–115
      email accounts, 118–119
      file formats, 260
      free space, 261
      music, 122–123
      overview, 139
      photos, 130–131
      podcasts, 124–125
      preventing iPad from syncing automatically,
        112–113
      sync conflicts, 260
      TV shows, 128–129
      videos, 122–123
    transferring purchased content to other computers, 141
    updating software, 246–247
iTunes U, 24
iWork suite
    buying, 23, 231
    components of, 22–23, 230–231

J

JavaScript, 70

K

keyboard dock, 6, 31, 75, 111
keyboards
    full-sized, 30, 75, 135
    on-screen, 75
Keynote app, 22, 230

L

Label screen, Contacts app, 189
labels, contact, 188–189
landscape orientation
    displaying photos, 19
    email, 17, 20, 75
    Notes app, 21
    overview, 75
links, emailing, 20, 100–101, 170–171
List view, Calendar app, 199
Load Remote Images switch, Mail, Contacts, Calendars
  screen, 107
locations. See also Maps app
    bookmarking, 29, 216–217
    finding unbookmarked quickly, 217
    returning from specified to original starting point, 213
    specifying, 29
    specifying locations without address, 212–213
    viewing contact, 29, 214–215
    viewing current, 28, 210
Lock Sounds setting, Sounds screen, 42
Lock Volume Limit option, iPod app, 147
lost iPod or iPhone, 219
Lyrics & Podcast Info setting, iPod app, 147

M

Mac
    configuring MobileMe synchronization, 224–225
    connecting iPad to, 110–111
    moving apps to iPad, 240–241

restarting, 259
    syncing apps to iPad from, 27
    syncing photos with iPad, 130–131
    waking up, 255
Mail Accounts check box, MobileMe preference pane, 225
Mail Address button, 90
Mail app. See also email
    connecting with services, 82
    deleting accounts, 83
    disabling accounts, 83
    overview, 20
    saving photos from attachments, 132
    setting up iPad-only accounts, 83
    specifying default account, 83
    switching accounts, 83
Mail Link to this Page option, 101
maintaining iPad
    backing up and restoring data and settings, 248–249
    battery life
        Bluetooth, 251
        extreme temperatures, 251
        GPS, 251
        screen brightness, adjusting, 250
        Sleep mode, 250
        Wi-Fi, 250
    updating software, 246–247
Maps app
    bookmarking locations, 29, 216–217
    contact addresses, 28–29, 187
    directions, 28, 211
    finding unbookmarked locations quickly, 217
    overview, 7
    returning from specified location to original starting
      point, 213
    specifying locations, 29, 212–213
    viewing contact location, 29, 214–215
    viewing current location, 28, 210
Mark as Unplayed option, iTunes, 125
Mark as Unwatched option, iTunes, 129
memory, 4, 261
Minimum Font Size option, Mail, Contacts, Calendars screen,
  102
Minimum Font Size screen, 103

Index

MobileMe
    finding lost iPod or iPhone, 219
    iDisk, 219
    publishing to MobileMe Gallery, 218
    sending photos to MobileMe Gallery, 228–229
    setting up accounts, 220–221
    setting up on PC, 226–227
    syncing
        configuring, 222–225
        overview, 218
MobileMe Gallery
    publishing to, 218
    sending photos to, 157, 228–229
    viewing without publishing, 229
MobileMe preference pane, 225
MobileMe Preferences dialog box, Windows, 227
MobileMe setup screen, 221
Mono Audio feature, 209
Most Viewed category, YouTube, 166
motion sensor technology
    email, 17, 20
    orientation, 75
    undoing pastes, 53, 55
    video games, 26
    viewing photos, 19
Move and Scale screen, 47
movies, 25, 152–153. *See also* videos
multi-touch screen
    full-sized keyboards, 75
    overview, 4–5, 16
    scrolling, 74
    tapping, 75
    zooming, 74–75
music
    buying, 24
    managing, 25, 123
    playing, 24
    syncing, 122–123
Music category, iPod app, 148
Music tab, iTunes, 122
Mute button, 5
My Info field, AutoFill screen, 77
My Videos option, YouTube, 167

N
Name field
    Add Account screen, 85
    New Account screen, 86
Names and Passwords option, AutoFill screen, 77
National Television System Committee (NTSC), 155
Network and Internet Connection options, Windows, 227
Network Settings, resetting, 257
network signal icon, 63
networks
    3G
        connecting to, 6
        managing data plan, 65
        monitoring data usage, 64
        overview, 4, 61
        roaming charges, 65
        signing up for, 64
    EDGE cellular technology, 61
    Wi-Fi
        connecting to, 6, 62–63
        overview, 4, 60
        troubleshooting, 256–257
        turning on/off, 45, 250
New Account screen, 86
New Mail setting, Sounds screen, 42
New Page option, Safari, 69
New Playlist dialog box, iTunes, 151
Notes app, 7, 21
Notes field, Contacts app, 193
Now Playing screen, iPod app, 149
NTSC (National Television System Committee), 155
Numbers app, 23, 231

O
On/Off, Sleep/Wake button, 5, 9
on-screen keyboard, 75
Outgoing Mail Server section, 87
Outlook, 227

P
pages
    creating, 11
    managing multiple browser, 17, 68–69
    scrolling through, 16

Pages app, 22, 230
Pages icon, 68, 69
PAL (Phase Alternating Line), 155
parental controls, 12, 48–49
Passcode Lock option, General screen, 38
Passcode Lock screen, 39
passcodes
    changing, 39
    forgotten, 49
    overview, 38–39
    parental controls, 49
Password field
    Add Account screen, 85
    New Account screen, 86
Paste button, 53, 55
pasting
    editable text, 52–53
    non-editable text, 52
    photos, 54–55
Phase Alternating Line (PAL), 155
photos
    albums, viewing, 18
    assigning to contacts, 19, 194–195
    copying and pasting, 54–55
    importing
        downloading images, 135
        overview, 18
        SD card reader, 135
        USB to Dock adapter, 134
    picture frame, using iPad as, 19
    saving from emails, 132–133
    saving from websites, 133
    scaling as wallpaper, 47
    sending by email, 19, 158–159
    sending to MobileMe Gallery, 228–229
    slideshows, 18, 160–161
    syncing on computer with iPad, 130–131
    viewing, 156–157
Photos app
    albums, viewing, 18
    assigning photos to contacts, 19, 195
    emailing photos, 19, 158–159
    importing photos, 18

picture frame, using iPad as, 19
    sending photos by email, 158–159
    sending photos to MobileMe Gallery, 228–229
    slideshows, 18, 160–161
    viewing photos, 156–157
Photos tab, iTunes, 130
Picture Frame feature, 19, 159
playing
    iPod content, 148–149
    movies, 152–153
    music, 24
    slideshows, 18
    TV shows, 152–153
    videos, 6, 152–153
playlists, 139, 150–151
Plus icon, address bar, 72
podcasts
    buying, 24
    designating as unplayed, 125
    managing, 25
    resolving problems with, 143
    subscribing to, 142–143
    syncing, 124–125
Podcasts tab, iTunes, 124
POP (Post Office Protocol), 83, 86–87, 94
pop-up blocking, 71
portrait orientation
    displaying photos, 19
    email, 17, 20, 75
Post Office Protocol (POP), 83, 86–87, 94
power-cycling, 253
Prevent iPods, iPhones, and iPads from syncing automatically
    check box, iTunes, 113
Price button, App Store, 238–239
Primary Server field, SMTP screen, 97
privacy options
    clearing History and cache, 71
    cookies, 71
    Fraud Warning, 70
protective cases, 30
Publish Photo screen, Photos app, 229
Purchased category, iPod app, 148
purchasing. See buying
push accounts, 93

Index

Push setting, Fetch New Data screen, 223
pushpins, Maps app, 29

R

rating
    iTunes content, 144–145
    YouTube videos, 165
Ratings For setting, Restrictions screen, 49
reading books, 173. *See also* iBooks app
Real Simple Syndication (RSS) feeds, 78–79
Recents list, Maps app, 217
Refresh button, Mail app, 98
Repeat Event dialog box, Calendar app, 200
replacing batteries, 252
Require Passcode option, Passcode Lock screen, 39
Reset All Settings option, Reset screen, 51
Reset Home Screen Layout option, Reset screen, 37
Reset Homescreen Layout option, Reset screen, 51
Reset Keyboard Dictionary option, Reset screen, 51
Reset Location Warnings option, Reset screen, 51
Reset Network Settings option, Reset screen, 51
Reset option, General screen, 36, 50
Reset screen, 36–37, 51
resetting
    devices, 253
    Home screen default layout, 36–37
    iPad, 50–51
    Network Settings, 257
    router, 257
restarting
    computer, 259
    devices, 253
    iPad, 258
restoring
    data and settings, 248–249
    default presets, 13
Restrictions option, General screen, 48
Restrictions screen, 48, 49
reviews, app, 235
roaming charges, 65
routers, 60, 257
RSS (Real Simple Syndication) feeds, 78–79
RSS icon, 79

S

Safari browser. *See also* Internet
    bookmarking favorite websites, 72–73
    managing multiple browser pages, 17, 68–69
    overview, 16
    search engines, changing default, 66–67
    security and privacy options
        clearing browser History and cache, 71
        cookies, 71
        Fraud Warning, 70
        JavaScript, 70
        pop-up blocking, 71
Safari option, Settings screen, 66
screen reader, 12, 208
screen saver, 159
scrolling, 74
SD card reader, 135
Search Engine option, Safari screen, 67
Search Engine screen, 67
search engines, changing default, 66–67
Search option, YouTube, 167
searching iPad, 56–57
security options
    clearing browser History and cache, 71
    cookies, 71
    Fraud Warning, 70
    JavaScript, 70
    pop-up blocking, 71
Selected albums and events, and automatically include radio button, iTunes, 131
Selected calendars radio button, iTunes, 117
Selected groups radio button, iTunes, 115
Selected playlist, artists, and genres radio button, iTunes, 123
selection box, 52
Sent Mail setting, Sounds screen, 42
Server Port option, 95
server ports, switching, 94–95
service appointments, 255
Set Both option, Move and Scale screen, 47
Set Passcode dialog box, 39
Set Passcode screen, 39, 49
Settings icon, 36
Settings screen, 38

Share button
    Mail app, 133
    Photos app, 159, 195, 229
Share option, YouTube, 171
Shuffle mode, 18
Sign In screen, iTunes, 141
Signature screen, 105
signatures, email, 20, 104–105
Simple Mail Transfer Protocol (SMTP) authentication, 96–97
Sleep mode
    configuring, 40–41
    manually entering, 41
    turning on/off, 250
    unlocking iPad, 8–9
Slide to Unlock screen, 8
slideshows
    creating, 160–161
    playing, 18
    setting duration of, 161
SMTP (Simple Mail Transfer Protocol) authentication, 96–97
SMTP screen, 97
Sound Check setting, iPod app, 146
sounds, turning on/off, 42
Sounds option, General screen, 42
Sounds screen, 42
speaker, 5
Spotlight
    capabilities of, 57
    searching iPad, 56–57
Spotlight screen, 56–57
Standby mode, 8
Start & End dialog box, Calendar app, 197, 203
Start Playing option, Video options, 155
Store option, iBooks, 174
subscribing
    to podcasts, 142–143
    to YouTube channels, 165
Subscriptions option, YouTube, 167
Summary screen, iTunes, 114
Summary tab, iTunes, 246–247, 248–249
Switch Start and End button, Maps app, 213
switching
    email accounts, 83, 90–91
    server ports, 94–95
Sync Address Book Contacts check box, iTunes, 115

Sync Apps check box, iTunes, 240
Sync AudioBooks check box, iTunes, 126
Sync bookmarks with check box, 121
Sync iCal Calendars check box, iTunes, 117
Sync Mail Accounts check box, iTunes, 119
Sync Music check box, iTunes, 122
Sync Photos from check box, iTunes, 130
Sync Podcasts check box, iTunes, 124
Sync Safari bookmarks check box, iTunes, 121
Sync selected mail accounts from check box, iTunes, 119
Sync TV Shows check box, iTunes, 128
Sync with MobileMe check box, MobileMe Preferences dialog, 227
Synchronize with MobileMe check box, MobileMe preference pane, 225
syncing
    apps, 27, 240–241
    audiobooks, 126–127
    bookmarks, 120–121
    calendar, 116–117
    connecting iPad to computer, 110–111
    contacts list, 114–115
    email account, 118–119
    iTunes
        automatic syncing, 261
        file formats, 260
        free space, 261
        sync conflicts, 260
    MobileMe
        configuring, 222–225
        overview, 218
    music, 122–123
    overview, 139
    photos
        on computer with iPad, 130–131
        importing from camera, 134–135
        saving from emails, 132–133
    podcasts, 124–125
    preventing iPad from syncing automatically, 112–113
    resolving problems with, 115
    sync conflicts, 115
    TV shows, 128–129
    videos, 122–123
System Preferences window, 224

Index

T

tapping screen
> double-tapping, 74
> one tap, 74
> tapping, holding, and dragging, 75
technical specifications, 4
television. *See* TV shows
templates
> Keynote, 22
> Numbers, 23
> Pages, 22
30-pin connector, 5
3G
> connecting to, 6
> managing data plan, 65
> monitoring data usage, 64
> overview, 4, 61
> roaming charges, 65
> signing up for, 64
Top 25 list, App Store, 235
Top Rated category, YouTube, 166
Tracking button, Maps app, 28, 210, 212
troubleshooting
> battery charging
>> cable connections, 254
>> service appointments, 255
>> USB ports, 254
>> waking up computer, 255
> connected devices
>> connections and power switches, 252
>> replacing batteries, 252
>> resetting devices, 253
>> restarting devices, 253
>> upgrading firmware, 253
> iTunes recognition of iPad
>> cable connection, 258
>> display, 259
>> restarting computer, 259
>> restarting iPad, 258
>> system requirements, 259
>> USB ports, 258
> iTunes syncing
>> automatic sync, 261
>> file format, 260

> free space, 261
> sync conflicts, 260
> Wi-Fi
>> Airplane mode, 256
>> antenna, 256
>> disconnecting and reconnecting, 256
>> range, 257
>> resetting Network Settings, 257
>> resetting router, 257
Turn Passcode Off option, Passcode Lock screen, 39
Turn Passcode On option, Set Passcode screen, 39
turning on/off
> Airplane mode, 45, 256
> AutoFill, 76–77
> Bluetooth, 251
> GPS, 251
> Sleep mode, 250
> sounds, 42
> Wi-Fi, 45, 250
TV shows
> buying, 24
> designating as unplayed, 129
> playing, 152–153
> syncing, 128–129
> viewing, 25
> watching on TV screen through iPad, 153
TV Shows tab, iTunes, 128
TV Signal option, Video options, 155

U

undoing pastes, 53, 55
Unlimited Data plan, 65
Unlock Volume Limit option, iPod app, 147
Updates screen, App Store, 242–243
updating
> apps, 27, 242–243
> software, 246–247
upgrading firmware, 253
URLs. *See also* links, emailing
> assigning to contacts, 184–185
> copying and pasting, 52–53, 101
USB keyboards, 135
USB ports, 111, 254, 258

USB power adapter, 31
USB to Dock connector, 27, 110–111, 134, 254
Use Contact Info setting, AutoFill screen, 77
Use Existing Account option, iTunes, 141

V

Verifying email account information screen, 85
video games
  downloading, 26
  playing on computers, 237
Video options, Settings screen, 155
video settings, 154–155
videos
  buying, 24
  comments, YouTube, 165
  emailing links to, 170–171
  groups, YouTube, 165
  locating, 166–167
  managing, 25
  playing, 6, 152–153
  saving as favorites, 168–169
  saving from attachments, 133
  sharing, 164
  subscribing to YouTube channels, 165
  syncing, 122–123
  viewing, 25, 164
Videos app, 152
viewing
  all appointments, 255
  contact location, 29, 214–215
  current location, 28, 210
  duration of events, 197
  email, 20
  photo albums, 18
  photos, 19, 156–157
  RSS feeds, 78–79
  videos, 25, 164
Voice Control screen, 8
VoiceOver feature, 209
Volume Limit setting, iPod app, 147
Volume Up/Down buttons, 5

W

wallpaper, 46–47
Wallpaper field, Brightness & Wallpaper screen, 46
Web
  3G
    connecting to, 6
    managing data plan, 65
    monitoring data usage, 64
    overview, 4, 61
    roaming charges, 65
    signing up for, 64
  assigning web address to contacts, 184–185
  bookmarking favorite websites, 72–73
  EDGE cellular technology, 61
  email, 17
    account settings, 91
    adding accounts, 84–85
    assigning addresses to contacts, 182–183
    authentication, configuring, 96–97
    automatically checking for messages, 98–99
    connecting with services, 82
    creating accounts, 86–87
    deleting accounts, 83
    disabling accounts, 83, 92–93
    disabling remote message images, 106–107
    font size, 102–103
    managing accounts, 20, 82–83
    overview, 17
    protocols, 83
    recognized services, 20, 82, 84
    reviewing with Outlook, 227
    saving photos from, 132–133
    security, 70
    sending links, 20, 100–101, 170–171
    sending photos, 19, 158–159
    server ports, switching, 94–95
    setting up iPad-only accounts, 83
    signatures, 20, 104–105
    specifying default account, 83, 88–89
    storing on server, 87
    switching accounts, 83, 90–91
    syncing accounts, 118–119, 139
    viewing, 20

Index

Internet Service Providers, 60
managing multiple browser pages, 17, 68–69
Safari browser, 16
search engines, changing default, 66–67
security and privacy options
    clearing browser History and cache, 71
    cookies, 71
    Fraud Warning, 70
    JavaScript, 70
    pop-up blocking, 71
Wi-Fi
    connecting to, 6, 62–63
    overview, 4, 60
    troubleshooting, 256–257
    turning on/off, 45, 250
web bugs, 106–107
White on Black feature, 209
Widescreen setting, Video options, 155
widescreen view, 6
Wi-Fi
    connecting to, 6, 62–63
    overview, 4, 60
    troubleshooting, 256–257
    turning on/off, 45, 250
Wi-Fi option, Settings screen, 45
wireless keyboards, 135
Write a Review option, iTunes, 145
Write a Review page, iTunes, 145

Y

Yahoo!, 67
YouTube
    comments, 165
    emailing links to videos, 170–171
    groups, 165
    locating videos, 166–167
    saving videos as favorites, 168–169
    sharing videos, 164
    subscribing to channels, 165
    viewing videos, 25, 164

Z

zooming in/out
    apps, 103
    with multi-touch screen, 16, 74
    photos, 157, 195
    for visually impaired, 208